MARXISM AND ETHICS

New Studies in Ethics
Edited by W. D. Hudson

What is involved in judging a person to be moral or immoral, or
in calling an action right or wrong? What makes a man good or
an action our duty? Such questions as these, which concern the
nature and content of morality, have been discussed by philosophers from earliest times and are still live issues today.

Many different types of ethical theory have emerged. New
Studies in Ethics meets the need for an up-to-date examination of
the main types. This series of monographs covers the whole range
of ethical theory from Greek philosophers to the latest develop-
ments in contemporary moral philosophy. Each study is complete
in itself and the whole series provides a unique treatment of the
main philosophical problems in ethics.

A distinguished team of philosophers, drawn from universities
in Great Britain, the U.S.A. and Australia, was invited to prepare
these studies. They have provided a series of monographs which
will prove indispensable to university students of Moral Philosophy, and will interest any intelligent reader.

The Series

Marxism and Ethics

EUGENE KAMENKA, B.A., Ph.D.

Professorial Fellow in the History of Ideas
Australian National University

MACMILLAN
ST MARTIN'S PRESS

First edition 1969
Reprinted 1970

Published by
MACMILLAN AND CO LTD
London and Basingstoke
Associated companies in New York Toronto
Dublin Melbourne Johannesburg and Madras

Library of Congress catalog card no. 69–13687

SBN (paper) 333 08864 6

Printed in Great Britain by
RICHARD CLAY (THE CHAUCER PRESS), LTD
Bungay Suffolk

CONTENTS

CONTENTS

EDITOR'S PREFACE

Dr Kamenka is one of the best-informed students of Marxism at present writing in English and he brings to this study of Marx's ethical teaching and its aftermath wide knowledge and critical acumen.

He has compressed a wealth of scholarship into narrow compass and provided an exposition and assessment of what Marx and some of his followers had to say on moral issues which is concise, clear and comprehensive. He puts the reader in a position to judge both the logic of Marx's arguments and the morality of the policies which he advocated on the strength of those arguments.

At least two features of the study will make it of particular interest to students of philosophy. One is Dr Kamenka's careful statement of the precise nature of Marx's humanism, a matter about which there has been some misunderstanding. The other is the way in which he brings out the connections between Marx's leading ideas and the work of other philosophers.

University of Exeter   W. D. HUDSON

ACKNOWLEDGEMENTS

Work on this study was begun in the Institute of Advanced Studies of the Australian National University in Canberra and completed in the Research Institute on Communist Affairs in Columbia University in the City of New York; I owe much to the excellent conditions for research and writing offered by both Institutes. Mrs E. Y. Short of the Australian National University gave me a great deal of help with bibliographical problems and references; I am very grateful to her. The Research Institute on Communist Affairs in Columbia University offered me a senior fellowship during my sabbatical leave (January 1968– January 1969) so that I might complete this and another study. Mrs Christine Dodson and the staff of the Institute have helped me to prepare the manuscript for publication.

EUGENE KAMENKA

I. INTRODUCTION

Readers of a series devoted to the various types of ethical theory from the Greeks to the present day may well have expected this component study to bear the simple title, *Marxist Ethics*. Such a title would have been misleading. Marx himself wrote nothing substantial or systematic on the problems of ethical theory or moral philosophy as such; his disciples, beginning with Engels, have distinguished themselves in this field mainly by their philosophical dilettantism and consequent *naïveté*. At a time when serious philosophers were beginning to see that further progress in ethics required careful logical analysis, the disentangling of issues and the solution of certain quite fundamental logical problems, Marxist writers approached the subject with complete disdain for technical questions and a fundamental inability to grasp the difficulty of the problems they were pretending to tackle. Much, indeed most, of their writing was popular in character and pamphleteering in spirit, directed against the moral pundit and the street-corner revivalist, against 'Christian' or 'bourgeois' ethics in their crudest form. In relation to the genuine logical concerns and insights of a Plato, a Butler, a Hume or a Kant most of the Marxist arguments were simply part of a tedious *ignoratio elenchi*.

The penalty imposed on the amateur is that he relives, unwittingly, the history of the subject. He sincerely presents as his own discoveries views that have already been held, elaborated, discussed and exposed at a higher level; he jumbles together what the professional, with care and devotion, has long since shown to be distinct and mutually inconsistent. Marxists, in fact, have failed to develop an original or comparatively coherent view of ethics that can be ranked as 'a type of ethical theory' finding its natural logical place beside utilitarian ethics, ethical intuitionism, existentialist ethics, or even Greek ethics. In the work of the

I

Marxists and, to a lesser extent, in the work of Marx himself, we find an uncritical conflation of ethical relativism, evolutionary ethics, the ethic of self-determination and self-realisation, utilitarian strains, the ethic of co-operation and a kind of social subjectivism, all assumed or proclaimed rather than argued for. The work of disentangling these strands, and of assessing the place of each strand in Marxist thinking about ethics, has been left almost entirely to those examining the Marxist position from outside. When such examination is carried out, the illusion of a coherent and worked-out Marxist position in ethics disappears, together with the illusion that the works of Marx and Engels, let alone those of their professed disciples, form a single and unambiguous intellectual system. We are left, as this study will attempt to show, with what is at most a number of insights, noticeably provided by Marx and not by his disciples. These insights might be relevant to someone else's attempt to deal with the problems of ethics in a serious and professional way. They constitute *reminders*, things ethical theorists should not forget, rather than propositions on which an ethical theory can be based. It is for this reason that I have chosen to call this study *Marxism and Ethics*.

To say that Marxism has nothing worthy of being called a serious position in ethical philosophy is not to say that ethics is peripheral to Marxism, or to Marx's own thinking about society. In a book written some years ago – *The Ethical Foundations of Marxism* – I attempted to bring out the ethical beliefs and hopes that lay at the centre of Marx's position and made him a radical critic of bourgeois society. Marx's primitive ethic, as I called it then, was in my view utopian and involved certain fundamental logical confusions, but it was by no means a mere set of unworked-out moral preferences and moral prejudices, as some of Marx's more old-fashioned or less scholarly critics sometimes still maintain. Marx's own ethical impulse stems from Rousseau and Kant and the ethic of German romanticism; his roots lie in an important ethical and intellectual tradition. As Marx the philosopher became somewhat submerged beneath Marx the social scientist this ethical impulse was to some extent hidden from view by accretions

2

from other sources – by the materialist critique of moralities, by Darwinian strains, by a concentration on material needs that bore a superficial resemblance to utilitarianism. To some, perhaps even to most, of his disciples, these accretions seemed the very essence of Marxist ethics. In this study I shall therefore attempt to combine history and analysis, a discussion of the varieties of ethic in Marxism with a discussion of the significance of Marxism for the theory of ethics. I shall distinguish between the various ethical strains found in the work of Marx and Marxists and between the various periods in the life of Marx and in the life of the movement erected in his name. We should especially guard against conflating and confusing the views of Marx with the cruder, more naïve versions of his thought publicised by Engels. The primitive ethic of Karl Marx and its revival in the current cult of alienation and the young Marx form the subject of Chapters II and III, the more traditional Marxist attempt to deal with ethics in terms of the 'materialist interpretation of history' is discussed in Chapters IV and V, while Soviet attempts to create a formal, philosophical discipline called 'Marxist ethics' are examined in Chapter VI. Marxism as a distinctive intellectual view is disintegrating in ethics, as in all other fields; it has left behind it a legacy of 'reminders' rather than a foundation for moral philosophy or a key to the solution of ethical disputes. The importance of these reminders at any particular time is directly proportionate to the social *naïveté* and lack of historical sense of those who write about ethics.

3

II. THE ETHICAL IMPULSE IN THE WORK OF KARL MARX

Until recently, the important implications of classical Marxism for moral philosophy have been taken to lie in its critique of objectivism in ethics, in its 'exposure' of the pretended impartiality and universality of moral injunctions and codes. 'Reason', Hume had said, 'is the slave of the passions'; morality, Marx and Engels appeared to be claiming, is the slave of interest. Marx's 'materialist' conception of history, according to his disciples, showed that moral codes and beliefs were man-dependent, born of man's social situation and varying as that situation varied. Since there was no 'man in general', since there were only specific men belonging to this or that specific social class, there was no morality in general. There were only specific *moralities*, reflecting the specific interests, demands and situations of specific classes, conflicting as these classes conflict. Moral codes or beliefs could therefore not be treated as true or false, valid or invalid, *in themselves*. They belonged to a particular historical time and expressed the concerns of a particular historical group; only in this context could they be understood and appraised. It was possible to speak in the name of the slave-owning morality or the slave morality, in the name of feudal morality, or bourgeois morality, or proletarian morality. It was not possible to speak in the name of *morality as such*; to do so was to utter nothing but empty sounds, to assert a common interest where there was no common interest, to speak in the name of a consensus when there simply was no consensus.

The rejection of any appeal to 'abstract' moral principles was for many decades one of the best-known features of the work of Marx and Engels. Marxism was distinguished from utopian socialism precisely by reference to its *scientific* character, to its refusal to confront society with moral principles and moral appeals. 'Communists preach no morality at all', Marx wrote (characteristically) in the *German Ideology* (1845–6).[1] 'They do not put to people the moral demand: Love one another, be not egoists, etc.; on the contrary, they know very well that egoism, like sacrifice, is under specific conditions a necessary [inevitable] form of the individual's struggle for survival.' Throughout the remainder of his life Marx would object bitterly to any attempt to base a socialist programme on 'abstract' moral demands embodied in such terms as 'justice', 'equality', etc. Marxism was a science; it did not advocate socialism, it showed that socialism was inevitable. It did not ask for a 'just' wage, it showed that the wage-system was self-destructive. Marxism did not confront society with moral principles, but studied the 'laws of motion' that governed social change. It did not tell the proletariat what it *ought* to do, but showed the proletariat what it would be *forced* to do, by its own character and situation, by its position in 'history'.

Moral philosophers, however, have long been aware of what seems to be an important underlying inconsistency in the Marxist view. Marxists, including Marx himself, have not merely predicted socialism, as a scientist might predict earthquakes, they have worked for the coming of socialism and made it clear that they will welcome its coming. They have been committed to the moral superiority of socialism over preceding systems. This *ad hominem* criticism can easily be supplemented by showing the same *prima facie* inconsistency in the theoretical writings of Marx and Engels. In the 'philosophical' writings of Engels, indeed, there is no doubt that the inconsistency is more than apparent. It breaks out sharply in the proclamation which Engels put side by side with his somewhat crude relativist treatment of moralities, the proclamation that proletarian morality is the ultimate, highest, 'truly human' morality destined to become the morality of all mankind. For Engels, it is clear, moralities do themselves progress; they pass, like society in general, through successively 'higher' stages until they reach the ultimate rational, truly human condition. Clearly implicit in all this is an (unexamined and unspecified) eternal, immutable, non-relativistic standard by which historical moralities are judged – precisely the sort of standard, in fact, that Engels has been concerned to reject. Karl Marx was too able and subtle a thinker to fall into Engels's flagrant inconsistencies;[2] we shall not find Marx obviously contradicting himself in the one breath. But it is clear that Marx, too, saw the coming society of Communism as ethically higher than its predecessors, even as the *first* truly ethical society. He was prepared to denounce exploitation, privilege, servility and the divided class society – though not the exploiters, the privileged, the servile, the classes themselves[3] – in terms which were unmistakably ethical, or at least moral-advocative, in tone. It has not always been clear to his critics whether Marx was implicitly appealing to a worked-out though unpublished ethic consistent with his exposure of class moralities and meant to supplement it, or whether he was merely giving vent to unexamined moral preferences and prejudices unaccounted for in his theory.

(i) DIFFICULTY OF INTERPRETATION

One of the great difficulties for the critic, as for the student wishing to tackle Marx's ethical theory seriously, is the lack of any extended or systematic discussion of ethics in any particular place in the whole corpus of Marx's work. An anthology entitled *Marx on Ethics* would contain no passages that continue to be strictly relevant for more than three or four sentences. The passages would come from diverse sources and unexpected contexts, making it hard to gauge their intended scope or to be sure that they are not polemical overstatements or simplifications. Marx, of course, had been educated as a philosopher, but with the 'discovery' of his materialist conception of history in the spring of 1845, followed by his collaboration with Engels on the *German Ideology* (1845–6), he wrote *finis* – it seemed – to the philosophical style and concerns of his youth. From 1848, when he was thirty, to his death in 1883, he devoted himself almost exclusively to his economic studies and to political pamphleteering and analysis. His style grew more empirical and his pretensions increasingly 'scientific' in the Comtean and Victorian English sense of the word. 'Philosophy' he left to Engels – unfortunately so, for it is

6

difficult to believe that anything other than Marx's great sense of material and psychological indebtedness to Engels's friendship, coupled with Marx's immersion in other work, can account for his failure to express dissatisfaction with Engels's performance or to repudiate Engels's claim to be presenting a joint view. From those of Marx's works that were known to socialists and social thinkers in the hey-day of classical Marxism between 1870 and the 1920s therefore, from such works, for example, as the *Contribution to the Critique of Political Economy* and *Capital*, the *Communist Manifesto*, the *Critique of the Gotha Programme* and *The Civil War in France*, one could only speculate concerning Marx's outlook on ethics, or on most other philosophical questions. The typical discussion of Marx's outlook on ethics in this period proceeded either by way of deduction from his general theory of history and society or by imaginative exegesis of a few scattered remarks. Then, in the late 1920s and early 1930s, came the first systematic publication of Marx's earlier and more philosophical writings and notes, sponsored by the Marx–Engels Institute and initially edited and planned by the serious and devoted Communist Marx scholar David Riazanov. The impact of these newly discovered or rediscovered writings, especially in the English-speaking world, was much delayed by the Nazi persecution of culture and cultured men, by Stalin's only significant 'contribution' to Marxist scholarship (the dismissal, arrest and execution of Riazanov) and by the difficulties facing international communication and scholarly discussion in the Second World War. In consequence, only in the 1950s and the 1960s has the significance of Marx's early writings been fully appreciated in any country, and only in the last few years have some representative selections from these writings become available in English. Especially important for an understanding of the ethical background of Marx's work are his doctoral thesis on the philosophy of nature of Democritus and Epicurus (1841), his incomplete critique of portions of Hegel's *Philosophy of Right* (1843), his contributions to the *Deutsch-französische Jahrbücher* of 1844 and the *Economico-Philosophical Manuscripts* that he jotted down later that year. It is in the light of these writings, many modern philosophical writers agree, that the ethic running through Marx's work is best understood, though the emphases to be placed on various strands and periods in Marx's work are – understandably enough – still the subject of dispute. There is especially sharp disagreement about the question of continuity in the development of Marx's thought, but this question, too, can now be approached much more knowledgeably and seriously through a consideration of the drafts, couched in remarkably philosophical language, which Marx prepared in 1857–8 while working on his *Contribution to the Critique of Political Economy*. These drafts, first fully published in two parts, in the original German, by the Foreign Languages Publishing House in Moscow in 1939 and 1941, were almost unnoticed at that troubled time. Their republication in East Berlin in one volume in 1953, under the 1939 title *Grundrisse der Kritik der politischen Ökonomie* has since brought them into the purview of Marx scholarship and has helped to demonstrate further that Marx took his early philosophical views on economics seriously well after he had become a Communist and a 'materialist'. A small section of the *Grundrisse* is now available for the English reader in the volume *Karl Marx, Pre-Capitalist Formations*, edited by E. J. Hobsbawm and translated by Jack Cohen, published in London in 1964.

(ii) MAN AS A 'SUBJECT'

Karl Marx [I have written elsewhere[4]] came to Communism in the interests of freedom, not of security. In his early years, he sought to free himself from the pressure exercised by the mediocre German police state of Frederick William IV. He rejected its censorship, its elevation of authority and of religion, its cultural Philistinism and its empty talk of national interest and moral duty. Later he came to believe that such pressures and such human dependence could not be destroyed without destroying capitalism and the whole system of private property from which capitalism had developed.

Professor Popper sensed the same moral commitment to freedom from a consideration of Marx's mature work alone.

Marx's condemnation of capitalism [he writes[5]] is fundamentally a moral condemnation. . . . The system is condemned because, by forcing the exploiter to enslave the exploited, it robs both of their freedom.

8

Marx did not combat wealth, nor did he praise poverty. He hated capitalism, not for its accumulation of wealth, but for its oligarchical character; he hated it because in this system wealth means political power in the sense of power over men. Labour power is made a commodity; that means that men must sell themselves on the market. Marx hated the system because it resembled slavery.

Marx's early writings have confirmed this. Underlying the whole of his work, providing the ethical impulse that guided his hopes and his studies, was a vision and a theory of human freedom, of man as master of himself, of nature and of history. It was a vision of the fully social man who has developed all his potentialities, made himself the aim and measure of all things, subsumed them to his human needs and purposes. It is this vision and this theory that modern philosophical writers refer to when they speak of Marx's *humanism* or, to emphasise the element of rebellion, of his *Promethean ethic*. This ethic was reinforced by Marx's leading character trait – his tremendous concern (in reaction against his prudent father and the humiliations invited by his Jewish origin) with *dignity*, seen as independence and mastery over obstacles. As late as 1873, asked to state the vice he detested most, Marx replied: 'Servility.' But this line also has its roots in the history of Europe, and especially in the history of Germany in the period 1770–1848.

As the scientific rationality of Western civilisation began to bear its full fruit [Professor Marcuse writes in an interesting work [6]] it became increasingly conscious of its psychical implications. The ego which undertook the rational transformation of the human and natural environment revealed itself as an essentially aggressive, offensive subject, whose thoughts and actions were designed for mastering objects. It was a *subject* against an object. This *a priori* antagonistic experience defined the *ego cogitans* as well as the *ego agens*. Nature (its own as well as the external world) were 'given' to the ego as something that had to be fought, conquered and even violated.

This concept of man as a *subject* – implicit, to some extent, in Cartesian philosophy with its sharp ontological distinction between consciousness and matter, that is, user and used – reached its first theoretical culmination in one strain in the philosophy of Kant. In the *Critique of Pure Reason* Kant had striven to show that

B

9

the necessary structure of the phenomenal world was imposed upon it by the knowing mind. Even the concept of God was merely one of the 'regulative ideas' of pure reason, a product of the rational mind's search for a single principle of explanation and for an ultimate unity in nature. In the *Critique of Practical Reason* he had argued that morality presupposes, behind the phenomenal human being subject to the laws of nature and of reason, a pure rational will moving freely in the intelligible, noumenal world. This will was self-determined, subject to no laws but the self-imposed rational law 'to treat humanity in every case as an end, and never as a means'. In the *Critique of Judgment* Kant had continued his vindication of man, attempting to show that man is the measure of all things beautiful, that aesthetic appreciation arises from the harmony between the object of cognition and the forms of knowledge. It is man, as the bearer of a rational faculty and as a knowing subject, who gives nature its supreme end and divine form, who organises its materials, and in morality proclaims himself as the highest end and being. Small wonder that Marx saw Kant as representing the French Revolution in the sphere of ideas, the declaration of the rights of man translated into philosophy (and thus made practically impotent). Two, three generations of young Germans, from Schiller and the young Fichte onwards, were to fight religious and political censorship and oppression in the name of the (Kantian) autonomy of man. Was it not Kant himself who had only one portrait in his study – that of Rousseau – and who was (wrongly) suspected of having written the young Fichte's *Critique of All Revelation*?[7] Did not the whole new moral critique of religion and the authoritarian state, from Fichte to Feuerbach, take its departure from the Kantian proposition that morality rests on the autonomy, religion (like political authoritarianism) on the heteronomy, of man? Was man the creator, the focal point of the universe, the condition of all knowledge, to be degraded into a dependent and externally determined creature? 'The criticism of religion' (i.e. Feuerbach's *Essence of Christianity*), the young Karl Marx wrote in the *Deutsch-französische Jahrbücher*, 'ends in the teaching that *man is the highest being for man*, it ends, that is, with the categorical imperative to overthrow all conditions in which man is a debased, forsaken, contemptible being forced into servitude, conditions which cannot be better portrayed than in the exclamation of a Frenchman at hearing of a projected tax on dogs: "Poor dogs! They want to treat you like men!" ' 'Punishment, coercion,' Marx writes in the Holy Family, 'is contrary to human conduct', because, as he had written earlier elsewhere, 'where the law is true law, i.e. the existence of freedom, it is the true existence of the freedom of man. . . . Law retreats before man's life as a life of freedom.' Or again: 'Every emancipation consists of leading the human world and human relationships back to man himself.' Or: 'A social revolution . . . is the protest of man against the dehumanised life . . . the fellowship against whose separation from himself the individual is reacting is the true fellowship of man, the fellowship of being human.'

This is not the place to go on multiplying texts from Marx in order to document, step by step, the development and the details of Marx's concept of the free man as the basis of ethics, philosophy and, ultimately, of the whole of social science.[8] Neither can we consider at all carefully here the materials from which Marx fashioned his doctrine, that is, the easily demonstrable influence on him of aspects of the thought of Kant and Fichte and, more obviously and directly, of the writings of Hegel, the Left Hegelians and Feuerbach. But in the formative years of his life, between 1841 and 1845, Marx did emerge with a doctrine that represented as worked-out a position on ethical philosophy as he ever reached, and which remained – I believe – implicit in the rest of his work, shaping not only his moral outlook, but his whole conception of human history, its problems and its destiny. That doctrine may be summarised as follows:

The presupposition and the true end of ethics, of philosophy, of all human activities, is the free, truly human man. Man is potentially the only subject in a world of objects, and anything that turns him into an object, subordinates him to powers outside himself, is inhuman. To Marx, as to so many other eighteenth- and nineteenth-century European radicals, there was something especially monstrous about an alleged type of self-abasement, about the situation in which man fell slave to things or institutions that he had *himself* created, to human forces severed from humanity, the situation in which man humiliated himself before an idol of his own making. This process Marx, following Hegel, called (self-)alienation and estrangement, or later, *fetishism* and *dehumanisation*, and it represented for him the ultimate in self-degradation. Ethics, for Marx, then, was concerned with freedom, and freedom meant human self-determination; it meant that man was governed by his own nature and its requirements, and by that alone. Man's nature consisted of a set of potentialities; freedom allowed him to go about the task of realising them to the full. It enabled him to subordinate nature and his environment to his will, to realise himself in work and in his intercourse with others instead of subordinating himself to demands confronting him as alien requirements, as limitations on his being and not as fulfilments of it. (This is what one can call the Kantian strain in Marx, though one must remember that it is a simplified, Prometheanised Kant – a Kant without the conflict between duty and inclination, without the frank elevation of the noumenal will over man's empirical nature, and without Kant's recognition of the independent requirements of logic or 'reason'.)

From the logic of Hegel Marx derived further content for the conception of freedom, and hence of the good. Conflict and 'contradiction' may be the necessary condition of change (and hence of progress), but they are also the marks of that inadequacy, one-sidedness, incompleteness which produces a necessary instability. 'That which is the Best', Marx had quoted approvingly (from Aristotle) in his doctoral thesis, 'has no need of action but is itself the end.' The truly harmonious, the stable, the ultimately durable, is the truly real as against that which is dependent and therefore to some extent unreal, contingent, temporary. To change in conflict is to be determined from outside; to suffer contradiction is not yet to be free. Thus 'contradictions' (practical and theoretical incoherence, conflict, instability) become for Marx moral criteria. The 'contradictions' of capitalism are not mere signs of its impending collapse, but also symptoms of its *in*humanity, of its (historically conditioned) failure to make the

12

free man, consciously controlling his fate, the basis of the whole system. The importance of this conception in Marx's thinking becomes evident when we compare his *Economico-Philosophical Manuscripts* of 1844 with an otherwise similar criticism of capitalist economics published by Engels a few months earlier, his 'Outlines of a Critique of Political Economy'. Engels's article, which Marx praised highly and which helped to bring about their friendship, criticised political economy both morally and logically – but the two criticisms were distinct. Marx, on the other hand, insists that ethical deficiency and logical 'contradiction' are necessarily connected. No criticism is complete until the two have been shown to arise from a single cause, a 'one-sided' treatment of man or a failure to grasp the human content of social and economic institutions. The whole point of the *Economico-Philosophical Manuscripts* is to proclaim that political economy cannot be an ethically neutral study of so-called 'objective relations' between non-human economic categories. The fundamental categories of political economy, Marx insists, are not labour, capital, profits, rent, land. The fundamental category is man, man and his human activities. These activities must not be abstracted from man; they must be seen as integral expressions of his humanity. It is when these categories are abstracted, objectified, reified, given independence vis-à-vis man, that man falls into servitude and the system of political economy into theoretical contradictions expressed in actual conflict and instability. Only by bringing economics back under the control of man can the subject be made coherent, the economic system stable and man become free.

What, however, of man's relation with other men? Here Marx begins with a (quasi-Hegelian) conception drawn from Feuerbach, that of man as a *Gattungswesen*, a species-being. In the *Essence of Christianity*, first published in 1841 and causing an immediate sensation, Feuerbach had argued that man cannot be treated as an abstract individual, in the way in which Christianity treats him. Human beings belong to one of two sexes, and the concept of 'humanity' cannot be accounted for, or formed, without recognising that any individual is *incomplete* as a human

13

being without another, especially of the opposite sex. Love, which Feuerbach treats as the central human characteristic, requires two people, an *I* and a *Thou*, and so does man's recognition of himself as a member of a species, as a universal and not merely a particular being. The distinctive species-characteristics of man cannot be imagined to exist unless there is a second human being in interaction with whom man develops love, speech and the knowledge of himself and his (common) humanity, that is, becomes human. Marx, who had no high opinion of Feuerbach's somewhat metaphysical preoccupation with love and sexuality, treats the concept of humanity more socially in the political sense of the word. Man is part of a community; he cannot do everything himself, he cannot realise his potentialities, or come to know his capacities, except in contact and co-operation with others. (Robinson Crusoe is logically possible only as a castaway, as one reared in society and *then* severed from it.) When society is truly human, other men appear before man as complements of his being, as collaborators in common human purposes, as 'himself once more'. Society becomes truly human when man ceases to be an abstract individual confronted by other abstract and therefore hostile individuals, when each man recognises himself as a universal, social being, a *Gattungswesen* in whom the community speaks and acts. For Marx, at least in 1844, this was what Communism was all about:

Communism . . . [is] the real *appropriation of the essentially human* by and for man; . . . the complete and conscious return of man to himself as a *social*, i.e. human, man. This Communism . . . is the genuine resolution of the conflict between man and nature and between man and man – the true resolution of the conflict between existence and essential being, between reification and self-confirmation, between freedom and necessity, between the individual and the species. Communism is the riddle of history solved, and it knows itself to be the solution.

What one is to make of all this we go on to consider in the next chapter.

III. ETHICS AND ALIENATION

The Marxian system, I have been arguing, begins with a 'philosophy of man'. It proclaims man to be the presupposition and the end of all philosophy, all science and all human activity; for Marx man is the *subject* in terms of which these latter are to be understood and judged. Ludwig Feuerbach, an understanding of whose earlier work forms an indispensable precondition for the appreciation of Marx's aims and methods, summarised his own philosophical development from his beginnings as a theological student, through his Hegelian period to his *Essence of Christianity* thus: 'God was my first thought, Reason my second thought, man my third and last thought.' In the *Essence of Christianity*, Feuerbach added: 'There is no other essence which man can think of, dream, imagine, feel, believe in, wish for, love and adore as the *absolute*, than the essence of human nature itself.'[9] Marx, as philosophical critics now increasingly recognise, took seriously and actually tried to carry out the programme which Feuerbach had only been able to sketch in his *Preliminary Theses for the Reform of Philosophy* – the dissolution of philosophy in its traditional (German idealist) form, its negation and preservation at a higher level in a new and complete *science of man* as a creative, social being, destined to become master of himself and the universe. Ethically, this means that, for Marx as for Feuerbach, man is the sole and ultimate standard, the absolute in terms of which all else is to be judged. ('Marxism', the Soviet philosopher A. M. Deborin wrote in 1923, 'is thus a variety of Feuerbachianism',[10] and the contemporary Polish Marxist, Adam Schaff, entitles his interpretation and defence of Marxism *A Philosophy of Man*.)

Professor Robert C. Tucker, in an interesting though often one-sided and philosophically cavalier book,[11] has argued that one necessary consequence of the Promethean ethic is a 'neurotic' bifurcation of man: the romantic, utopian (according to Tucker, typically *neurotic*) elevation of man as subject, creator, Absolute (which can only take place in fantasy) brings with it a strongly emotional (neurotic) rejection of man's actual life in the real world; empirical man is felt to be dependent, forsaken, humiliated, frustrated, fallen from grace. Whatever we may think of Tucker's charge of neurosis, it is certainly true that this *is* how Marx portrays man in this world. The servitude of man in all past human societies and the coming liberation from this servitude provide the basic plot of the Marxian conception of history which is a moral drama (though it is not only that). Those things which Marx sees as enslaving man are the primary targets of Marx's criticism and the main object of his study.

(i) THE ROLE OF MONEY

'The critique of society which forms the substance of Marx's work', a leading French Marx scholar, Dr Maximilien Rubel, correctly reminds us,[12] 'has, essentially, two targets: the State and Money.' The State, for Marx, was the visible, institutionalised expression of political power over men; money, both the visible means and the secret but indispensable ground of the more fundamental and pervasive economic power over men. If Marx was concerned with the critique of politics and economics, it was because he saw in these critiques the key to understanding the human condition and grasping the necessary foundations for the elimination of power over men. Throughout his work, Marx makes it clear that he does not see man enslaved simply by other men: the citizen by a dictatorial police state, the worker by a greedy and grasping capitalist. All past and present social systems may resolve themselves, from one point of view, into systems made up of masters and slaves – but the masters are no more free than the slaves, both live in a relationship of mutual hostility and of insurmountable mutual dependence, both are governed by the system that makes them play out their allotted roles, whether they will or not. Marx sees this dependence as arising 'naturally' from the division of labour and the consequent introduction of private ownership. But the possibilities of intensifying dependence, of alienating man from his work, his products and his fellow human beings, are vastly increased with the rise of money as a universal medium of exchange. Money – into which everything can be converted – makes everything saleable. It enables man to separate from himself not only his goods, the product of his work, but even his capacity to work itself, which he can now sell to another.

Money lowers all the goods of mankind and transforms them into a commodity. Money is the universal, self-constituting value of all things. It has therefore robbed the whole world, both the human world and nature, of its own peculiar value. Money is the essence of man's work and existence, alienated from man, and this alien essence dominates him and he prays to it.[13]

Man's alienation, for Marx, is expressed in the fact that man's forces, products and creations – all those things that are extensions of man's personality and should serve directly to enrich it – are split off from man; they acquire independent status and power and turn back on man to dominate him as his master. It is he who becomes their servant. As the division of labour, the use of money and the growth of private property increase, man's alienation becomes more acute, reaching its highest point in modern capitalist society. Feudalism enslaved the whole man; capitalism splits man's functions off from man and uses them to enslave him. In capitalism the worker is alienated from his product, from the work that he sells on the 'labour market', from other men who confront him as capitalists exploiting his labour or as workers competing for jobs, and from nature and society which confront him as limitations and not as fulfilments of his personality. It is this alienation – expressed in the intellectual field by the compartmentalisation of the science of man and society into the 'abstract' study of economic man, legal man, ethical man, etc. – which Marx portrays vividly in his *Economico-Philosophical Manuscripts*:

The more riches the worker produces, the more his production increases in power and scope, the poorer he becomes. The more commodities a worker produces, the cheaper a commodity he becomes. The devaluation of the world of men proceeds in direct proportion to

17

the exploitation of the values of the world of things. Labour not only produces commodities, but it turns itself and the worker into commodities. . . .

Not only the products of man's work, but the very activity of this work are alienated from man. The alienation within the worker's activity consists:

First, in the fact that labour is external to the worker, i.e. it does not belong to his essential being, in the fact that he therefore does not affirm himself in his work, but negates himself in it, that he does not feel content, but unhappy in it, that he develops no free physical and mental energy but mortifies his body and ruins his mind. Therefore the worker feels himself only outside his work, while in his work he feels outside himself. He is at home when he is not working and when he works he is not at home. His work, therefore, is not voluntary but coerced; it is *forced* labour. It is, therefore, not the satisfaction of a need, but only a means for satisfying needs external to it. . . .

The result therefore is that man (the worker) no longer feels himself acting freely except in his animal functions, eating, drinking, procreating, or at most in his dwelling, ornaments, etc., while in his human functions he feels more and more like an animal. What is animal becomes human and what is human becomes animal.

Drinking, eating, and procreating are admittedly also genuinely human functions. But in their abstraction, which separates them from the remaining range of human functions and turns them into sole and ultimate ends, they are animal.

At the end of his *Economico-Philosophical Manuscripts* of 1844, Marx painted a picture of the Communist society, the society of true and ultimate human freedom. Sympathetic critics have called it the picture of a society of artists, creating freely and consciously, working together in spontaneous and perfect harmony. In such a society, Marx believed, there would be no State, no criminals, no conflicts, no need for punitive authority and coercive rules. Each man would be 'caught up' in productive labour with other men, fulfilling himself in social, co-operative creation. The struggle would be a common struggle: in his work, and in other men, man would find not dependence and unpleasantness, but freedom and satisfaction, just as artists find inspiration and satisfaction in their own work and in the work of other artists. Truly free men rising above the very conception of property will thus need no rules imposed from above, no moral exhortations to do their duty, no authorities laying down what is to be done. Art cannot be created by plans imposed from outside; it knows no authorities and no discipline except the authority and discipline of art itself. What is true of art, Marx believed, is true of all free, productive labour. Just as true Communism, for Marx, is not that crude Communism which 'is so much under the sway of *material* property, that it wants to destroy everything which cannot be owned by everybody as *private property*; it wants *forcibly* to cut away talent, etc.'; so free labour, for Marx, 'is not mere fun, mere amusement, as Fourier thinks with all the *naïveté* of a *grisette*. Truly free labour, for example, composition, is damned serious at the same time, it is the most intensive exertion.'[14]

(ii) FOUR ASPECTS OF ALIENATION

Alienation for Marx, then, occurs when man falls into servitude to and dependence upon his own powers or the institutions and goods he has himself created; it is overcome when man makes all his activities free expressions of his nature and full satisfactions of his needs. In its consummate form (i.e. in bourgeois society), alienation takes place at four levels, or in four ways:

(1) Man is alienated from the things he produces and his own labour in producing them. Instead of serving his needs, these come to dominate him and his life. (Marx, in the conditions of his time, would have taken as an example the seamstress, whose life is determined by and is an adjunct to the need for producing dresses, instead of the production of dresses being determined by the needs of the seamstress.) Socialists today often use as an example the cult of mass consumption and built-in obsolescence, the manipulation of the consumer to buy and to orient his life to buying, because in our economic system 'things demand to be bought', production needs more and more consumers, not because anyone thinks the *consumer* needs the things produced.

(2) Man is alienated from other men through the competitive character of the economic system based on private property, which forces everyone to live at someone else's expense and

which, in particular, divides men into classes with irreconcilable interests. Man's fellow-beings therefore confront him as *hostile* beings; they *limit* his exercise of his capacities instead of extending it.

(3) Man is alienated from nature, which does not confront him as a field for the creative exercise of his powers, but as a source of difficulty and drudgery, as a limitation on his creative powers.

(4) Man is alienated from society as the expression of social, collective power. In so far as a political interest is possible in capitalist or any class society, it confronts men as an external, separate interest, as the state interest distinguished from and conflicting with private interests. (It is in reflection of this that moral rules appear as external, alien rules laid down by a 'higher' authority.)

Alienation in the practical, 'material' life of man is reflected in man's theoretical life, in the creation of 'abstract' sciences such as traditional philosophy, economics, ethics, etc. Each of these sciences deals with a feature of man or of human activity in isolation, as though it were independent of the whole man and his entire social history and circumstances. It thus subjects man to 'laws' that stand outside himself – to the law of barter, which is one law, to the law of morality, which is distinct and separate from it, to the laws of reason, treated as eternal and immutable and 'above' man's actual wants and desires. Each of these 'abstract' sciences, as the young Marx – following Feuerbach – would have put it, takes one of man's predicates and converts it into a subject, tears it out of the context without which it cannot be understood.

We are now in a position to see how Marx could resolve the apparent tension between his ethical vindication of Communism – his man-centred ethico-logic – and his materialist critique of moralities. The materialist conception of history, at least in its emphasis on the historical laws that determine man's development independently of his will, is the law of man's development in the *period of alienation*, in what the later Marx called the prehistory of mankind. Moralities are sectional, class-bound, conflicting, dependent on economic interests, not truly ethical or truly human, because *man* is still sectional, class-bound, in mutual conflict, dependent on economic interests and not truly human or free. As long as man cannot be himself, as long as man is forced to play out a social role cast for him by the system, he cannot become the subject of ethics. His moralities are not expressions of his humanity, but reactions to his (inhuman) condition; individuals are not ethically culpable because their actions are not free, they are forced upon them by the conditions of their life. When man recognises the inhumanity of his condition, he leaves behind the field of moralities and enters upon a human ethic; he stands on the threshold of consciously gained and consciously exercised freedom; he becomes an ethical subject who judges himself by the standards of his own nature instead of being a moral object judged by external standards imposed upon him.

Viewed as a *morality*, judged in terms of its ethical *content*, the Marxian proclamation of the moral primacy of man obviously forms part of an important (modern) moral tradition. It is not the mere personal eccentricity of some romantic philosopher, fallen under the spell of Hegel and Feuerbach and taking it upon himself to project on to man the qualities that past generations had thought to be typically and exclusively proper to God. Marx's view has strong and deep roots in the culture created by the Reformation and strengthened by the scientific and industrial revolutions; it is an extreme, radical, thoroughgoing expression of that elevation of man and his concerns that began with Luther, gained strength with the French Revolution and forms the basis of most 'progressive', social democratic and ethical humanist agitation and reform since the revolutions of 1848. It is the implicit assumption behind the intensified struggle for religious and political liberty, and social and economic dignity, which marks off the modern from the medieval world. It is, and has been, especially effective wherever the impact of science, education and technical progress is vitiated by political and religious impediments to modernisation, where man's actual subordination to authority and need is felt to be sharply, intolerably at variance with 'the human spirit', with man's potentialities as the user of science and technology, as the destined sovereign of nature and free creator of literature and art. This is why Marxism has appealed especially to the intelligentsia – the rather special class produced by the (limited) spread of knowledge and education from industrial societies into backward, traditional, agrarian societies in which knowledge and education of the western kind act as revolutionary forces and their bearers become a special revolutionary class. It is not surprising either, then, that Marxian humanism has had an important impact on the intellectuals of Communist-dominated eastern Europe, where Party control and authority are felt to provide such impediments. Nor is it surprising that it has had far less direct impact in Communist China and much of the rest of Asia and Africa, where the belief in man's unlimited potentialities is still basically weak, where moralities, outlooks and expectations are still in the main pre-industrial, and where nationalism is currently a *substitute* for humanism. Marxian humanism shares the man-centredness of utilitarian ethics, but it is much more effective than utilitarianism in registering protest against those conditions in which modernisation is hindered (as in India) by the continuing modesty of human wants, by the self-imposed limitation of desires and expectations, by the acceptance of hardship, suffering and waste of human resources as 'natural'. For utilitarianism takes the desires and expectations of man at any given moment as an ultimate; Marx's morality seeks to transform and 'enrich' his wants, to increase his expectations, to prevent him from finding 'happiness' by tailoring his demands to his satisfactions, by learning to like what he gets. Utilitarianism works within a given social and political system and criticises it only where it fails to satisfy demands expressed within the system; Marxian humanism is prepared to transcend the system, to criticise the system itself for the wants and demands it creates.

In recent times, especially in advanced industrial countries and among men whose outlook was moulded by the horrifying excesses of Hitler and Stalin, there has been a marked revulsion from the Promethean ethic of human liberation on the ground that it provides no in-built check against such horrifying excesses. In the work of Karl Popper, with its emphasis on the dangers of historicism and utopianism and its vindication of piecemeal social engineering, in the 'Christian realism' of Reinhold Niebuhr, in the political theory of Michael Oakeshott, this revulsion has provided the psychological impetus and political foundation for a return to 'the ethic of prudent mediocrity' of a Burke, a Pope or a Goethe. Man's potentialities are for great good or for great evil; it is best if he does not become drunk with his own power, but proceeds little by little, respecting the actual, empirical desires of others and keeping within rules meant to restrain his passions and his experiments. This is the – anti-Promethean – message of a great deal of contemporary moral and political writing. It appeals greatly to the increasing number of (middle-class non-'coloured') men who are reasonably comfortable in their own existing society and believe in the capacity of a system that has institutionalised change and technological progress to deal with strains and injustices without major dislocation or revolutionary outbursts.

For the moral philosopher, however, the historical popularity or unpopularity of Marx's ethic and its relation to types of society and social change is not the main point. Moral philosophy, notoriously, is plagued by certain fundamental logical problems – the problem of the status and character of ethical propositions and of the nature and foundations of moral argument or justification. For some moral philosophers, too, the *raison d'être* and the final test of a moral philosophy lie in its ability to provide rational, convincing and workable criteria for resolving the problems of choice, for enabling men to choose among possible alternatives within a given human situation. 'To preach morality', Schopenhauer wrote, 'is easy, to give it a foundation is difficult.' Does Marx succeed where others have failed?

It is quite clear that Marx does not see ethics as providing a set of rules or criteria by which men can resolve the dilemma of moral choice in their day-to-day lives in society as we know it. 'Rights and duties', Marx wrote in the *German Ideology*, 'are the two complementary sides of a contradiction which belongs only to civil society' (i.e. to the society in which men pursue individual interests in conflict with each other and have not yet internalised the concept of community or created the material foundations for

23

such a community). As long as men face moral uncertainties, dilemmas of choice, they are facing situations that are inherently evil, situations in which interests conflict, in which one satisfaction can only be gained at the expense of another. The moral dignity of man requires something other than principles of arbitration between competing interests and demands, something other than principles which assume the existence of conflict and evil. Man's dignity requires the *overcoming* of those situations in which interests conflict, the creation of a society in which men have common purposes and agree naturally and spontaneously, as members of a family or a collective (allegedly) might agree, on what is to be done. Morality is not a question of rules, but a question of habits. Truly moral habits can only arise when man is free, free of superstition and external compulsion, free of the pressure of divisive classes and interests, free of property and free of compelling, soul-destroying need or the fear of need. True morality, in fact, is what free, rational, self-determined men acting without external compulsions would do. If there has been no true, spontaneous, natural morality in the past, this is only because men have never been able to realise themselves in free, rational, uncompelled social activity.

Marx thus attempts to sidestep the whole problem of justification in morals and the conflict between 'ought' and 'is'. Morality is not a question of what 'ought to be done'. The logical dilemma faced by moralists arises from the fact that they are trying to impose external principles of co-operation on societies that are by their nature incapable of producing spontaneous, rational and lasting co-operation, or from the fact that they abstract men and human activities from concrete social situations and lay down rules and requirements that ignore the realities of human life in that situation, ignore what a concrete man needs and can do. The reader should note the extent to which this view of Marx's is in tune with much of modern criminology, with the treatment that most sensitive contemporary writers give to juvenile delinquency or the 'culture of poverty'. 'Where the necessities of life are absent', the ageing Feuerbach wrote in the 1860s, long after Marx had ceased to read him, 'there [the consciousness of] moral necessity or obligation is also absent.' Moral indignation, as Feuerbach and Marx both saw, certainly comes most easily to those who are capable of treating the whole of mankind as though it were made in their own image and placed in their own (usually comfortable) situation. To say 'it is no use preaching at the juvenile delinquent, the point is to remove the poverty, sense of deprivation, alienation from the rest of society that produce the vast majority of delinquents' is to concede the validity of much that Marx is saying.

Nevertheless, Marx is not merely giving us a sociology of morals. Implicitly, at least, he is trying to justify his passionate and advocative pleading by pretending that his moral distinctions are in fact logical distinctions, that the denial of his morality would be the self-contradictory rejection of logic. He does not say this explicitly, but he creates an aura of logical necessity by the use of such terms as 'essence' (distinguished from mere 'existence'), 'truly human' (distinguished from empirical man), 'pre-history' (distinguished from 'true history'). It is this conception of a 'true' man, a 'true' history and a 'true' reality which is quite vital to Marx if he is to elevate a certain way of life, or a certain way of behaving, above others. This position rests on the (false) Hegelian idealist view that ordinary, empirical reality can somehow be logically deficient, lacking true or real reality. This logical deficiency, for Marx as for Hegel, is expressed in 'contradiction', where such contradiction is not true logical contradiction at all, but the existence of conflict and the empirical lack of complete self-sufficiency. To say that man, in his present state, is not 'truly human' is not to make a logical point but to make a moral one, to set up moral criteria of humanity that do not follow from the mere use or meaning of the word 'man'. In other words, Marx, like many moralists, is driven from the postulation of moral hierarchies to a postulation of logical hierarchies, to the conception of good as a 'higher', 'more real' type of existence.

Many critics have drawn attention to features of the Marxian view of history that raise the suspicion that it is an Hegelian theodicy, portraying mankind as evolving towards an ultimate messianic kingdom and history as containing a moral and logical

C

end to which all else is a necessary but in itself inadequate and incomplete prelude. Certainly Marxism is one (particularly subtle) version of the cult of the perfectibility of man and of progress in history, and the arguments that could be opposed to such optimism are never seriously examined, in fact hardly even conceived of. But more fundamental than the conflation of the historical and the moral end (which is more blatant in the writings of Engels and of Stalinist Communists than in the writings of Marx) are the confusions inherent in Marx's conception of man as destined to become the *subject* of history. Here Marx, through Hegel and other sources, has clearly been influenced by scholastic logic. Man, as Marx in his metaphysical moments portrays him, is (potentially) the *unconditioned being* of the scholastics (i.e. God), whose unconditionedness is one of his *perfections*, essential to his (true) nature, and therefore to be deduced from it. It is from the scholastic view of God that Marx unconsciously derives the conception of man as (properly) always a subject and never a predicate. It is from scholastic logic that he gets the otherwise unsupported notion that the self-sufficient, the self-determined, the always active, is morally superior to the conditioned, the determined, the also passive.

Now the simple answer to this is that man is neither wholly active nor wholly passive, neither (by his nature) always subject nor always predicate, neither self-determined nor wholly determined from outside. As the later Marx saw much more clearly, man interacts with his environment; he determines (affects) it and it determines (affects) him. That it is morally better to act than to be acted upon is never, in Marx or anywhere else, more than an unsupported assumption. It is not an uncommon assumption (providing one basis for feelings of male superiority and an ethic for Milton's Satan), but it is no better established for all that. There is nothing to show logically, without moral assumptions, that it is 'human' to act and 'inhuman' to be acted upon or even to be treated as a means or object; it is not 'contrary to human nature' to make oneself a beast of burden, an object of pleasure or part of the rat-race. Men and women have done so for many generations; to say that in doing so they have behaved as though

26

they were not human is to load the term 'human' with a moral content that cannot be deduced from its empirical denotation.

Marx's difficulties in this connection come out clearly in his treatment of 'alienation' as a fundamental ethical concept. It was a happy accident (and one that has proved rather temporary) that Marx could run together, in dealing with the vast mass of European mankind, dependence on wage-labour and the capitalist system, extreme poverty and suffering, and a feeling of utter lack of control over the conditions of one's life and work. For Marx, in consequence, several possible meanings of alienation became fused and blurred, even though Marx had himself admitted that the alienation which produces a feeling of misery and denial of his self in the worker produces a feeling of well-being and self-affirmation in the capitalist. In one sense of alienation, man is alienated whenever his actions, his circumstances, his whole life are determined by circumstances beyond his control. We have argued that such circumstances will always exist, that man can never be entirely self-determined. Alienation in this sense, therefore, is not 'alienation', a particular (evil) state of existence, but is simply what is naturally involved in all existence, which is always conditioned and never unconditioned. A second, somewhat less obviously utopian sense in which Marx seems to use alienation is when man's purposes are not determined by himself. Man's actions, even within the limitations set by events completely beyond human control, are not expressions of his desires, they are forced upon him by his external situation. But here, too, one has to say that there is no logical distinction between human purposes and human actions and conditions: what a man wants or purposes, as Marx himself argued, is the product of the man's past history and his environment, of the interaction between his character and his surroundings; our purposes are our own only in the sense that it is we who have them, not in the sense that they spring entirely out of an internal, self-contained history. If our purposes are to be looked at *objectively*, then they are never self-determined in the causal sense; they are only self-ratified, if you like, and such ratification also has a causal history. We are thus, in the objective sense, all alienated in all our purposes. Marx cannot attempt to avoid this difficulty by treating alienation *subjectively*, as so many contemporary American sociologists do, and as Marx himself does in emphasising the worker's *feeling* of dehumanisation. It is possible to draw a distinction between men who *feel* that their purposes are their own and men who feel that they are dominated by circumstances or other people or 'the system'. It may then be an empirical fact that the former feel satisfaction in their lives and the latter do not. (This would be a matter for empirical investigation; Marx avoids the need for this by linking alienation with poverty, which is no longer plausible.) But the whole point of Marx's critique is to discount the subjective criterion of the worker's feelings, to say that the slave is no less a slave because he feels himself to be free. Marx's whole argument, then, rests on his vacillation between the various possible meanings of alienation or on the implausible view that the three stand in relations of mutual implication. Even then, it requires for its moral impact and initial plausibility a further unsupported assumption. This is the assumption that from the point of view of ethics, of human freedom, there is a crucial distinction between limitations that result from 'natural' necessity and limitations that result from the actions of other human beings, whether they confront the individual as the demands of other people, of impersonal institutions, of social forces or of machines and commodities. Even if it were true that many men felt such a distinction to be morally relevant, this might be merely the result of romantic illusions, of their reluctance to concede that objects and institutions created by men acquire a life of their own. *Fetishism*, one might argue, lies not in being dominated by machines, but in thinking that because they were built by humans machines should somehow remain human, or subject to human control. Behind all this, one suspects, lurks another fallacy of scholastic logic, the view that the effect is somehow contained in, and properly subservient to, the cause. This accounts for one invalid argument of remarkable longevity, that children should respect their parents because the parents gave birth to them, and for another more modern version, that it is monstrous for man to be governed by machines because he made them.

For most people, without doubt, Marx's contribution to ethics will be most seriously vitiated by the patent utopianism of his conception of the truly human society with its spontaneous co-operative morality. The basis on which Marx predicts the flowering of such a morality is at times viciously metaphysical, at other times embarrassingly slender. Marx's confidence seems to rest on a mixture of the following propositions, each of them false:

(1) Man, when truly and fully human, when conscious of his nature, his potentialities and his relations with other men, is naturally co-operative. In Marx's early work this rests on a confused logical doctrine – the notion that an essence is truly universal and that man, in recognising his essential humanity, therefore necessarily recognises all other human beings as aspects of himself, or as himself once more and cannot, from his humanity, derive any ground for conflict with them. In Marx's later work, there is some, rather half-hearted, attempt to deduce such co-operation from the requirements of modern industry and to argue empirically that industrial workers are beginning to display such 'natural' co-operation. Engels, half-supported by Marx in the *Critique of the Gotha Programme* – as though conscious of the weakness of this – ultimately seems to come down on the view that the *abundance* of material goods produced under Communism will remove the grounds for conflict – as though men quarrelled only over material goods and as though marginal wants did not acquire greater urgency as other satisfactions come to be taken for granted.

(2) Man, in becoming truly human, is able to exercise untrammelled rationality. Given the common human purposes that Marx assumes, reason can and does provide the basis for complete agreement on all questions, from the allocation of resources to the priority of tasks. It is in line with this that Marx speaks, in the Preface to *Capital*, volume 1, of all social relations under Communism becoming rational and intelligible relations.

(3) All social conflicts can ultimately be derived from the institution of private property and the class structures created by it. With the abolition of that institution social conflict loses its

essential base. It is this which leads Marx to the view that in a society in which private property has been abolished and its existence forgotten the State, law and the criminal will wither away, men will see in each other their natural collaborators and colleagues and significant social conflict will become impossible.

For the philosopher all this, without question, will not do. Nor is it particularly convincing for the social theorist, who is well aware of the conflicts and tensions within and between those countries that have abolished private ownership of the means of production. And despite the popularity of the concept of alienation in recent radical writing, it seems to me clear that it is a concept useful to the moralist, to the littérateur and social critic, rather than to the serious ethical theorist. It is a dramatic way of bringing out the disparity, in contemporary post-industrial society, between man's technological and scientific powers and his ever-increasing degree of social dependence; it is also a way of liberating socialism from the necessity of predicting poverty. But in so far as the use of the term 'alienation' implies that such a disparity is somehow unnatural or in a more than moral sense inhuman, it is simply wrong. Alienation, in other words, is not a logical concept or a category on which a theory of ethics can be founded without further examination and analysis; in Marx and recent neo-Marxists it is a moral-advocative term deriving its force from moral assumptions it does not seriously examine and from the disparity between existing social conditions and some of the hopes and expectations born of the optimism of the scientific and industrial revolutions. This is not to say, of course, that any given society must be accepted as it is; it is to deny that logic and the nature of man prove it ought to be different. Let us admit frankly that moral and social reform are political activities, springing from and utilising existing (strictly historical) expectations, traditions and moral attitudes with their allied frustrations and dissatisfactions. To be morally adult is to be able to take a stand without demanding that history and logic be rewritten to support it, without demanding that the nature of the universe guarantee our 'rightness' and/or our prospects of success.

'A philosophy of man', Adam Schaff writes,[15] 'can start off from two opposite principles: (1) that man's existence is the realisation of some superhuman conception of plan, external to man; (2) that man's existence is the creation of man himself – man makes himself, and the starting point of all considerations about man should be that he is autonomous.' The upshot of our criticism of the young Marx's humanism was to deny that these *are* the two alternatives for a consideration of man's position, either logically or ethically. Man's existence is neither the realisation of some superhuman conception, nor is it the work of man himself. To use Hegelian language, man is both subject and predicate. There is no logical discontinuity between man and his environment, no actual or ideal truly human and unconditioned essence against which the whole of empirical human existence is to be set and judged. Human nature, human purposes and human conceptions are the product, at any given stage or in any given place, of the continuous interaction between actual existing men and their environment. They are to be understood neither in terms of 'man' alone, nor in terms of his environment alone. Man is thus neither autonomous nor heteronomous; what he is, at any time in history, is neither his own work nor that of another. While we can say that there are certain (e.g. physiological) features of man that have changed less drastically in the last two or three thousand years than other (e.g. cultural) features, there is no basis for proclaiming the existence of an underlying human nature that persists through and underlies all change and seeks to determine it. Such a human nature would have to become, like 'substance' in Locke, 'an uncertain supposition of we know not what', an empty and question-begging set of potentialities knowable only after the event.

Marx himself, in the 'materialist interpretation of history' which he develops after 1845, helps to lay the foundations for our criticism. 'All history', he argues against Proudhon in the *Poverty of Philosophy*, 'is nothing but the continuous transformation of human nature.' In notes criticising Feuerbach that he jotted down a little earlier (the *Theses on Feuerbach*), he writes: 'Feuerbach resolves the religious essence into the human. But the essence of man is no abstraction residing within each individual. In its real form, it is the ensemble of social relations.' In the *German Ideology* he elaborates: '[The] sum of productive forces, forms of capital and social forms of intercourse which every individual and generation finds in existence as something given is the real basis of what the philosophers have conceived as "substance" and "essence" of man.' Man is born into a specific society which shapes his outlook, capacities and hopes – he cannot be understood or discussed apart from the social arrangements in which he lives and the place which he occupies within those arrangements. Thus Marx went on to argue, in passing, in 1848, that 'conscience is related to the knowledge and whole way of life of a man. A Republican has a different conscience from a Royalist, a propertied man has a different conscience from one who is propertyless, a thoughtful man a different one from a man without thought.' In other words, as we suggested at the opening of this study, there is not morality, there are historically conditioned *moralities*. Conscience, Reason and Will are not ahistorical faculties confronting man as the voice of an inner essence or a transcendent truth; they are human functions and activities, products of the continuous interaction between changing men and their changing environment. It is precisely for this reason that each generation and social group reinterprets the meaning and significance of human history and of special histories – the history of philosophy, of science, and so on – in terms of the concerns, insights and attitudes born of its own historical situation, and it is for this reason that seemingly dispassionate, disinterested and well-informed men find themselves engaged in far-reaching moral and intellectual conflict.

Marx's naturalism, however, as we have hinted, was never

completely thoroughgoing; behind his materialist treatment of man the older Marx still strove to maintain his youthful belief in man as the ultimate subject in terms of which everything was to be understood. Thus Marx insists, with Vico, that man makes his own history; thus Marx attacks, in the *Theses on Feuerbach*, all previous materialism for treating the material world as given, for failing to see it as the product of human praxis; thus Marx ends with the slogan that man's task is to revolutionise and humanise the world: so far, 'philosophers have only interpreted the world differently, the point, however, is to change it'. Because Marx is wedded to the view that man is the ultimate ground and point of all history and existence, even his materialist account tends to emphasise the social (human) as against the natural (non-human); he is much happier reducing an intellectual phenomenon to a social situation (classes and economic production) than seeing it as the product of a natural (e.g. geographical) situation. There are times, notably in his account of despotic Asiatic society and in his acceptance of the 'mongolising' and 'tartarising' influence of the Russian terrain as a reason for Russian backwardness, when Marx does concede and use the direct influence of the natural world in shaping man. But generally, and in terms of his theory as a whole, Marx is anxious to avoid any form of direct geographical determinism (such as we find in Plekhanov) or any account in which man figures purely as an object acted upon by something else than other men and human products. Man's relation with 'nature' for Marx is always dialectical; man shapes it as it shapes him, there is no understanding one without the other. For Marx nothing that enters into relationship with man remains simply non-human. This is why the motive forces in the Marxian conception of history are characteristically human products – inventions and the class struggle, not rivers, mountains, trees or fields, which to Marx are nothing until they become objects of human intentions and purposes. Here the influence of classical idealism, with its view that mind permeates 'nature' and thus gives it significance and form, is still strong, though Marx's transformation of the doctrine makes it much more concrete, plausible and intellectually fruitful.

33

Nevertheless, in its most general tendency, Marx's materialist interpretation of history might well be taken as laying foundations – when taken together with the work of Feuerbach, Darwin and Freud – for a *naturalistic* view of man, for the recognition that man occupies no special logical place within historical, empirical processes and that he is neither logically nor causally discontinuous with them. The study of the human is not logically different from the study of the non-human; social development is not in principle different from non-social development. Man is part of the subject-matter of zoology, biology, physics and chemistry just as he is part of the subject-matter of economics, politics, sociology and the history of culture. He is *part* of these subjects and not a manipulator or organiser or 'presupposition' or 'end' standing outside them. The notion that man's purposes are independent ultimates controlling his life and his history is an illusion: we can study human purposes just as we study the purposes (drives and reactions) of primates or any other living organisms. While purposes may be causes, they are also effects. With the decline of mechanism, unfortunately, these have once again become (in different formulations) controversial questions among philosophers. In recent writing – in the work of such philosophers as Ryle and the later Ayer – they have been discussed at a level of sophistication and with an emphasis on close analysis undreamt of by Marx and ignored by his more recent disciples. It is not likely that any competent philosophers will find in Marx and the Marxists new insights into the logical problems raised by such recent writing. But it is important to beware of the unexamined and highly questionable assumptions that underly much of the new scholasticism – with its manipulative view of logic, its instrumentalism in relation to language and its extreme individualism in ethics and politics. Marx helps to remind us that human history creates a *prima facie* case against these assumptions, that they may be and have been questioned with force and insight.

At the same time, the materialist interpretation of history, with its emphasis on historical change and class conflict, helped to lay the foundations for pluralist view of man and society – for the recognition of competing moralities and outlooks within society and within the individual man himself. It taught us that society was not a harmonious whole and that men were not harmonious wholes. Just as there was no total social interest, subsuming and reconciling all individual interests, so there was no total individual interest – a man could be part of many traditions, confront himself and others in many roles, be torn between allegiances to competing groups and ways of life. Marx himself and his disciples, it should be noted, were never thoroughgoing in this pluralism: they did tend to treat any individual man as belonging to a single class and to think of society as being made up of a finite number of classes. Marxian pluralism has to be, and has been, carried further than Marxists have been willing to carry it: we have to recognise the individual man, and the individual society, as infinitely complex, as the battle-site of an infinite number of traditions, outlooks and ways of life, as an *economy* of motives and interests which can never be exhaustively enumerated. None of the components of such an economy can be treated as atomic simples, confronting other components as monads without windows. Within each society there is an infinite number of sub-societies; component traditions and interests have points of affinity as well as points of conflict; they enter into alliances, change allegiance, split up into further components and so on. The complexity of individuals and 'their' interests has long been recognised in literature, especially in the novel; it is time that it was more clearly recognised in ethics.

If the materialist interpretation of history has helped (primarily non-Marxists) to work towards a philosophy of naturalism and pluralism, it has had a seriously stultifying effect on the further working out of such a philosophy, especially among Marxists, and as much in the field of ethics as anywhere else. One of the well-known *misuses* to which the materialist interpretation was put was to substitute a genetic account of the origin of a view, or a reference to the interests it allegedly serves, for examination of the truth or falsity or internal coherence of the view itself. Thus an attempt to supplement 'scientific Marxism' with neo-Kantian morality might be denounced as 'petty bourgeois', or philosophers, scientists and historians might be attacked, as they were under Stalin, on the grounds of their 'class-origin'. (The most important fact about Berkeley, in Stalinist writings, was his being – in fact becoming – a bishop, and Russell was for years treated as an aristocrat philosopher.) The view that intellectual enquiry was itself necessarily the battle-ground of competing class-bound ideologies not unnaturally helped to introduce the dishonesty of political polemics into Marxist intellectual production and to create an atmosphere (amid the conditions of sharp political struggle) in which labelling a view as 'bourgeois' was an acceptable substitute for serious criticism. It was this trait which turned the work of so many able socialist writers into little more than political pamphleteering, and which makes the reading of most Marxist writing on ethics between 1880 and 1950 such an unrewarding task.

The position here was further obscured by Engels's proclamation, in his *Ludwig Feuerbach* and his *Anti-Dühring*, that all truth is relative. Engels's discussion is a particularly confused one and cannot be recommended to any serious student of philosophy for its contribution to the problem. Engels confuses absolute truth in the sense of what is unambiguously so or not with 'absolute truth' in the sense of complete knowledge, the sum of all possible knowledge. He concludes from the fact that we cannot ever exhaust all possible knowledge and that we can find later that our knowledge was 'inadequate' (or false), that we cannot ever say 'X is (absolutely and unambiguously) Y'. He has to concede, of course, that we do assert some propositions to be true *absolutely*, unambiguously, without a 'later-developing false side' but – he says – they are always trivial. Now, if propositions cannot in principle state an unambiguous issue, then we cannot talk or discuss at all.[16] It should be said, however, that this kind of relativism can be put forward more coherently in the field of ethics. If we leave aside the Marxist commitment to an ultimate morality, or an ultimate moral end, we might treat the materialist interpretation of history (especially in Engels's hands) as saying that there are no ethical truths – there are only moral outlooks. Such outlooks are produced historically – they are the outlooks, interests, demands of specific social groups (classes) in specific periods. It makes no sense to ask whether they are true or false. We can only ask what conditions produced them, what makes people subscribe to them, what conditions militate against their continued importance in society. In other words, we should treat moralities as we treat religions (other than our own) – as wishes, illusions, fantasies, demands, that acquire independent force, clothe themselves in principles, institutions, enforcement agencies, take up associated empirical material, etc. This is the view that I have referred to as a kind of social subjectivism, and that has also been called ethical relativism. It is popular among anthropologists, who do in fact treat the moral codes of the peoples they are studying in precisely this way. It has recently been defended again in Professor D. H. Monro's *Empiricism and Ethics* and seems to me to be a possible and coherent basis for approaching the problem of ethics. It is inconsistent with other aspects of Marxism, but it is not inconsistent in itself. The apparent objectivity of morals would, on this view, be an illusion – stemming from the fact that our moral outlook is not an individual creation but 'forced upon us', as it were, by our education, our social background, our immersion in various activities and ways of life. The sociologist Émile Durkheim, in his book *The Elementary Forms of the Religious Life*, gave one such naturalistic account of the feeling of transcendence, of objectivity, associated with moral beliefs. He saw it as resting on the recognition that the tribe precedes the individual and will go on after him, and that tribal ceremonies produce in the individual feelings, ecstasies, etc., beyond his conscious control. For the working out of details in this way, then, we once again have to look outside Marxism.

There is one other point of ethical interest suggested by the materialist interpretation of history which again has not been developed by Marxists themselves. (It was taken up, or at least hinted at, in the work of the French syndicalist Georges Sorel, with his distinction between the producers' morality of heroic dedication, work for its own sake, co-operation and emulation, as distinct from the prudential, utilitarian, competitive and individualistic morality of the consumer concerned with profit and reward, seeing all activities as means to an individual end.) This is the suggestion that moralities and moral demands are not those of individuals or groups of individuals, but the demands and requirements of a productive process or of a social activity, which carries with it certain norms in which people are caught up as part of carrying on the activity and which they come to accept as their own. (We do speak of the morality, or outlook, of military officers or commercial salesmen and of the morality, or outlook, of academic enquiry.) The existence of moralities as moralities required by an *activity*, or social province, in which individuals are caught up, is widely recognised in literature and in much political and historical writing, but it has not made the impact it should have made on ethics and political philosophy. There the tendency is still to think of the individual, and not of an activity, as the bearer of a morality and the subject of rights.

All this, however, is to look at the materialist interpretation of history imaginatively, a way in which orthodox Marxists have not looked at it. To them, it has been a 'law' of historical development and a canon of historical explanation; a reductive theory that provides a simple but complete and adequate account of morality and of all other ideological phenomena. As such, it derived what plausibility it had from the considerable ambiguity with which it was formulated and the noteworthy lack of precision or consistency in the way in which it was applied. True, Marx and Engels seemed to think that the whole thing came down to a simple preposition enunciated by Marx in the introduction to his *Contribution to the Critique of Political Economy*: 'the mode of production in material life determines the general character of the social, political and spiritual processes of life'. Within this material process of production Marx (and Engels after him) distinguished two separate, if related, factors: the *productive forces* and the *relations of production*. The productive forces are the skills, knowledge and tools (all of them social products) existing at any given period of society. The relations of production are the ways in which different factors of production (land, domestic animals, tools, machines, labour) are appropriated and in which economic returns are secured – in other words, the class structure of society

38

Systematising and bringing together various scattered remarks by Marx and Engels, subsequent Marxists (Plekhanov and Kautsky) expressed the theory thus: each society has an *economic base*, consisting of productive forces and relations of production. The state of development of the productive forces determines the relations of production, the class structure of a society. This class structure (or, in an alternative formulation, the economic base as a whole) determines the *superstructure*, the political and legal arrangements, moral, religious and other ideological beliefs of the society. As it changes, they change. In line with this, Marx and Engels wrote in the *German Ideology*:

Morality, religion, metaphysics, all the rest of ideology and their corresponding forms of consciousness thus no longer retain the semblance of independence. They have no history, no development; but men, altering their material production and their material inter-course alter – along with these – their real existence and their thinking and the products of their thinking.

The proletarian, Marx and Engels said in the *Communist Manifesto*, sees law, morality and religion as 'so many bourgeois prejudices, behind which lurk in ambush just as many bourgeois interests'. And a few pages later they added:

Does it require deep intuition to comprehend that man's ideas, views and conceptions, in a word, man's consciousness, changes with every change in the conditions of his material existence, in his social relations, and in his social life? What else does the history of ideas prove, than that intellectual production changes its character in pro-portion as material production is changed? The ruling ideas of each age have ever been the ideas of its ruling class.
When people speak of ideas that revolutionise society, they do but express the fact that within the old society the elements of the new one have been created, and that the dissolution of the old ideas keeps even pace with the dissolution of the old conditions of existence.

Completely in line with this Engels was to write many years later, in *Anti-Dühring*:

We maintain . . . that all former moral theories are the product, in the last analysis, of the economic stage which society had reached at that particular epoch. And as society has hitherto moved in class antagonisms, morality was always a class morality; it has either justified the domination and the interests of the ruling class, or, as soon as the oppressed class has become powerful enough, it has represented the revolt against the domination and the future interests of the oppressed.

There have been remarkably few sustained Marxist attempts to apply this doctrine in detail to ethical theories and the history of moral philosophy. Engels, in *Anti-Dühring*, gives a rough and unconvincing sketch in which he distinguishes Christian-feudal morality (subdivided into Protestant and Catholic moralities and into further subdivisions that Engels does not attempt to connect with class structure at all), bourgeois morality and 'the proletarian morality of the future'. He concedes that there are some moral injunctions, such as 'Thou shalt not steal', which are common to all periods of history in which society is based on private property, precisely because these periods have the existence of private property in common. Karl Kautsky, in his *Ethics and the Materialist Conception of History*, makes an honest but dilettantish attempt to take the Marxist account of morality seriously and apply it *in concreto*. He turns his attention to classical Greek moral philosophy. In the ancient world, he argues, the ethical question first emerged clearly as a result of the class tensions that followed the Persian wars. These wars placed the Greeks at the centre of widespread commercial activity and produced three leading types of morality: the Epicurean, representing those connected with private production; the Platonic and Neo-Platonic, representing the section of the aristocracy not engaged in personal control of production; the Stoic, representing several of the remaining classes and acting as a mediating ethical theory. (The logical concerns of the *Republic*, of course, or of the *Euthyphro*, find no real recognition in Kautsky.) Since then, we rarely meet with any Marxist analysis of the connection between a moral theory and a class position more profound than a reference to Aristotle's contempt for slaves and women or to Locke's exaltation of private property. (Professor I. S. Narsky, of Moscow, has just reminded us, in an otherwise serious book on Hume, that Hume's moral theory should be seen as Whig and not as Tory, as though that helped us to understand the subtle manner in which Hume wends his way between utilitarianism, a theory of moral sentiment and the requirements recognised by a man with an acute eye for logical difficulties.)

This lack of concrete application of the materialist interpretation of history should not cause surprise. It is precisely in the process of concrete application that the theory loses its plausibility and that the ambiguities in it become apparent. Marx himself, as I have striven to show elsewhere,[17] sat to it very loosely indeed in his own detailed account of economic history and in his political analyses and intellectual criticism. A number of recent critics have shown very clearly the difficulties and imprecision involved in the notion of an economic base to be distinguished from an ideological superstructure. Not only can we show, as Engels admitted and later Marxists now again admit, that ideological factors can and do react back on economic production and technical organisation. We can show even more fatally, as John Plamenatz did in his *German Marxism and Russian Communism*, that the distinction between the economic base and the ideological superstructure simply cannot be drawn in the way required by the theory. Ideological factors do not merely act on the base, they become part of it (feudal law is essential to the definition of feudal classes, for example). The 'base' thus becomes simply the whole social situation in which a person or movement finds itself. This can be demonstrated from the few concrete remarks that Marx and Engels make about moralities. It is never made clear precisely what they are to be reduced to or precisely what they 'express'. In the *Communist Manifesto* and in Engels's *Anti-Dühring* intellectual theories – especially law, political philosophy and ethics – are reduced directly to class interests, but what such interests are and precisely how they would be determined is never discussed. In his well-known epigram on Kant, on the other hand, Marx reduced Kant's doctrine of the good will not to the hypocritically concealed interests of the German bourgeoisie but to its *political impotence* coupled with its *aping of the French model* – that is, to the 'conditions' of the class, conditions in which 'material' and 'non-material' factors are jumbled together and no social factor is in principle excluded. Elsewhere – in the *German Ideology*, as we have seen – Marx goes beyond classes altogether by reducing the conflict of rights and duties in moral theory to the incoherence of a civil society based on private property and 'abstract' individuals. And in his theory of ideologies generally Marx seems to vacillate between treating ideologies as expressions of social interests on the one hand, and as compensations, fantasy-supplementations of social reality, on the other.

The materialist interpretation of history, in its allegedly concrete formulation, then, does not provide us with a key to the problems of moral philosophy. It may help us to ask questions; it does not itself provide any satisfactory answers. Anyone tightly bound to its dogmas is unlikely to find real answers. The history of moral philosophy *does* have a certain integrity: there are logical problems in ethics that worried a Plato, a Butler, a Hume, a Kant and a G. E. Moore independently of their moral sympathies. These logical problems cannot be removed or side-stepped merely by reference to the class-allegiance these philosophers had or to the conditions in which they lived. (It is when we believe the philosophers to have been wrong that we look for the distorting influence of time and place.) If moralities are to be interpreted as systems of demands or attitudes (which *are* historically conditioned, and the 'truth' or 'falsity' of which is not at issue), then the account to be given of them will have to be very much subtler and more careful than that suggested by the materialist interpretation of history or given by any Marxist. The distinction between moral demands and other demands has not been discussed by Marxists in any illuminating way; the foundation on which moral demands arise or the interests which they express has not been stated clearly. The complexity of moral beliefs and of problems about morality has simply not been recognised by Marxists. Those who want to work out a subjectivist ethic based on social movements and groups rather than individuals will have to go well beyond Marxism and discard much of it. Those who believe in an objectivist ethic will find nothing in the materialist interpretation of history that *proves* them to be wrong – though it does raise a strong presumption against the belief that there is an unhistorical voice of Conscience, or Reason, or the Good Will, that men have heard even if they have not heeded it. And Marxists themselves cannot proclaim ethical relativism in the same breath as that in which they set up the moral duty to the Revolution and the 'truly human morality' of socialism. This latter inconsistency only Marx himself avoided, and not always clearly.

V. HUMAN WELFARE AND HUMAN NEEDS

'Marxist–Leninist ethics', says a Soviet textbook on the subject,[18] 'also contains a normative aspect. It not only explains the social essence of morality and the laws of its development, but also provides a theoretical foundation for the moral goal of Communist society, for the norms and principles of Communist morality.' In other words, it gives ethics a *foundation* in Schopenhauer's sense; it allegedly provides a 'scientific' principle of justification for Communist morality. (In the Russian text, the Hegelian word *moment* is used where I have put 'aspect'. The use of this word makes it clear, and is meant to make it clear, that the normative aspect of Marxist–Leninist ethics is no accidental accretion, but an essential phase or aspect in Marxist–Leninist ethics, one that helps to determine its structure and development.)

Such a claim to derive normative principles from the Marxist science of society immediately attracts the attention of the moral philosopher and causes him unease. We have argued that the materialist conception of history, modified, reinterpreted, 'diluted' to a sociological naturalism, can be used to develop an internally consistent relativist or subjectivist view of ethics. On this view, 'moralities' would be ideologies in the strict Marxist sense, projections – in universalised or distorted form – of particular historical interests or demands, or empirical wishes that social life and human relations might be otherwise, or – most plausibly – a combination of both. Marxists would thus deny, as they have indeed often denied, that imperatives can ever be other than hypothetical, that the dictates of conscience or morality can ever be treated as eternally valid absolutes, that *values* exist independently of valuations. Such ethical relativism, however, seems at best difficult to reconcile with belief in the *objective* moral superiority of socialism, in the scientific basis (i.e. justification) of

Proletarian or Communist morality, or in moral progress (a conception which seems to imply underlying or meta-criteria logically independent of the actual historical moralities judged in terms of these criteria). While clear differences of approach to this problem can be detected among Marxists, both today and in the earlier history of Marxism, it is generally true that the issues involved have not been clearly grasped or distinguished by Marxists. The resultant tendency has been to have things all ways, to emphasise different approaches at different stages of the one work, and to say that they are all part of Marxism. The prestige of science in the late Victorian era and the first decades of the twentieth century led western European Marxists in the social democratic tradition to come down most heavily on the scientific, 'value-free' pretensions of Marxism. Thus the Austro-Marxist Rudolf Hilferding distinguished between *Marxism*, a *science* of society predicting the coming of a Communist society, and *socialism*, a *moral outlook* that welcomed this coming. Others, for example, Kautsky and Bernstein, were led to a 'moral supplementation' of Marxism – Kautsky by taking from Darwin an evolutionary ethic, Bernstein by appeal to the Kantian and neo-Kantian principle that all men must count equally and that man must never be used as a means. The Communists, concerned with revolutionary struggle and Party authority, tended to make their norms even more frankly imperative on the one hand but even more flexible on the other. True morality lay in obeying the dictates of history; since history was working towards the Revolution, the primary moral imperative was to aid the Revolution. In the light of this end, all else was to be judged. A gun, as Trotsky put it, is good in the hands of a proletarian fighting for the Revolution and evil in the hands of a *bourgeois* opposing it.

The point, however, is whether Marxists can with any plausibility derive such norms from the Marxist science of society and its 'materialist' conception of history. There are, in effect, only two ways in which this has been seriously attempted. One way was by arguing that norms are implanted in, or provided by, history itself. The other consisted of seeing man as the 'scientific' foundation for norms. The approach by way of history need not delay us long, though it was for many years the most influential and widespread approach within Marxism. It drew for authority primarily on Engels, who had conflated Darwin and Hegel (and in the process vulgarised Hegel and his dialectic into a doctrine of evolutionary progress through conflict and contradiction). To Engels, each stage of historical development was, at least in some respects, 'higher' than that which preceded it and the final stage of history was therefore the highest of all – an implicit end towards which all history, blindly and unconsciously, had been working. (It was in just this way that Darwinians saw man as the Crown of Creation, the *end* towards which evolution had unconsciously worked and in which it had surpassed itself. It should be noted, however, that this strain is also present in Hegel and Marx, even if it is expressed less simple-mindedly than in Engels.)

The difficulty here, of course, is obvious – in what sense, other than 'later', is each stage of history 'higher' than its predecessor? In moral Darwinism, notoriously, 'better' really meant only 'fitter to survive under given conditions' and in Hegel the slogans 'whatever is real is rational' and 'world history is the world court of justice' seemed, to a careless reader, pompous ways of saying that whatever triumphs is right. To show that the later is *morally* better, we should need an independent criterion in the light of which historical stages are judged. Hegel and the young Marx had such a criterion, whatever difficulties it may in turn raise. Engels did not, at least explicitly. When he writes, in *Anti-Dühring*, that in the process of historical change 'there has on the whole been progress in morality, *as in all other branches of human knowledge*' (my italics), he characteristically misses the point. We may be able to make some sense of the notion that later *science* is higher than earlier science – that is, that it incorporates, amends and corrects the knowledge gained by the former, and adds more knowledge. But how a series of *relativistic* moralities (expressions of interests, not truths) can suddenly become *truths*, or how one interest can be higher than another, is not shown and cannot be shown without making independent moral assumptions. Surely the whole point of Engels's preceding paragraph had been that each morality is *not* a branch of knowledge, but an ideology.

46

The appeal to man remains, then, as the only possible solution. An increasing number of Marxists, indeed, are taking this path – not only such quasi-Marxian humanists as Marcuse and Fromm, and the Yugoslav philosophers, but also such contemporary 'old-style' Marxists as Howard Selsam and Donald Clark Hodges, not to speak of the 'socialist humanism' now proclaimed by Soviet propagandist philosophers. Here the argument would run something like this: Man, as an empirical being, has certain purposes, needs and requirements which form part of the description of man and which must be recognised by any science that has man for its subject. Man's moral demands are the attempts to fulfil these requirements, to realise these needs. Provided the attempts are realistic and take into account objective conditions and realities, they are norms that any detached, honest and impartial human enquirer must accept as built into the nature of man. There is no point in asking for some further, metaphysical criterion by which man's requirements can be shown to be good – there is, after all, no ultimate or absolute for man more ultimate or absolute than his own needs.

This approach may be put more metaphysically (generally by those under the influence of the young Marx) or less metaphysically (by those who see themselves as 'materialists'). Marcuse attempts to ground the humanist ethic in logic by arguing that 'man' as a class-concept or universal necessarily involves criteria or principles by which we distinguish the human from the non-human. 'Man' is thus a normative concept from the start; to describe or define man is already to recognise goals towards which man works or ends towards which he strives. One such normative defining characteristic, emphasised by both Marx and Marcuse, is *consciousness* – for both, man is not truly human until he is able to act consciously, rationally, in the full knowledge and understanding of what he is doing. (Engels's use of the Hegelian slogan 'Freedom is the insight into necessity' is connected with this view of man.) Anything that interferes with man's exercise of his rationality thus makes man to that extent non-human and is therefore bad. On this view, there could be progress in morality, the progress consisting in its increasing rational practicality, its increased understanding of obstacles to the satisfaction of human needs and of the means that will result in the removal of such obstacles.

The more empirical Marxists tend to come much closer to utilitarianism, to think primarily in terms of happiness and suffering, satisfaction and deprivation, though also maintaining the emphasis on consciousness and practicality. Thus Adam Schaff writes:

> Scientific socialism is essentially humanist, and the essence of its humanism is its conception of the happiness of the individual. Everything in Marxism – its philosophy, political economy and political theory – is subordinated to this. For Marxism is the sum of theoretical instruments which serve one practical aim, the struggle for a happier human life. This is how Marx understood the question while still young, when he said that a revolutionary philosophy is the ideological weapon of the proletariat. Such is the meaning of the Marxist postulate of the unity of theory and practice. And this is why the theory of happiness takes on a specific form with Marxism – not as the abstract reflection of the meaning of happiness or of its subjective components, but as the revolutionary idea of that transformation of social relations which would make possible the creation of the conditions for a happy life by removing the social obstacles to such a life. Marxist socialism approaches the problem of individual happiness from its negative side, that is to say, it investigates the social obstacles to human happiness and how they can be removed. It is this approach which brings positive results, because of its realism.[19]

Howard Selsam, in his *Ethics and Progress*, puts it thus:

> The warp of ethics lies in man's ability to see a contradiction between what he is, how he lives, and what he could be and how he should live.[20]

> Throughout the world men are today turning away from old established standards and are creating richer, fuller human ethics by envisioning and seeking a life free of poverty and ignorance and offering the fullest possible development of man's limitless potentialities. Men make their moral codes and their ethical theories, and in the world today masses of people are making them, consciously or unconsciously, with blood and sweat, and with a deeper, securer sense of what human life on this earth should be than in any previous period of the world's history.[21]

Donald Clark Hodges, in a lengthy discussion of my *Ethical Foundations of Marxism*,[22] modifies some of his earlier pronouncements on Marx's ethics and now argues that Marxism provides no philosophical foundation for ethics, just as it itself does not rest on any ethical foundation. Marx is merely a sociologist of morals and a social critic who shows people how their moral demands can be satisfied. But Hodges, too, goes on to write:

One difference between the materialist and idealist approaches to human conduct is that the former bases itself upon the economic interests of individuals, which are necessary conditions of the full flowering of the personality, while the latter bases itself upon abstract principles, feelings and imaginary projections that provide little more than psychological comfort and the illusion of personal integrity. For those who have made their accommodation to poverty, as for those who have adjusted to physical and mental illness, self-interest consists in preserving the *status quo*. However, such people are not qualified judges even of their own interests. To judge one's own interests correctly is tantamount to knowing the assumed or conventional limits. Although disagreements arise from efforts to moderate conflicting aims and to implement them in the face of concerted opposition, there is much less reason for disagreement by qualified judges concerning the desirability of various forms of economic, social and political advancement over corresponding forms of degradation. As Engels notes in a critique of the humanistic ethics of Feuerbach, the happiness of man depends not upon moral but upon material considerations, especially economic instrumentalities, including the leisure affluence affords for enjoying members of the opposite sex, books, conversation, art, music, outdoor activities, and the like. . . . Instead of a moral struggle to rise above the pressures of the social environment, it is far more consonant with self-interest to struggle to bring economic and social conditions into conformity with human needs.[23]

The reader will hardly have failed to notice the tangle of unexamined moral-philosophical presuppositions that runs through this type of Marxist writing. There is a clear assumption of a life 'proper to man', constantly appealed to but quite inadequately discussed. In spite of all the play with empiricism, there is the distinction – made explicit by Hodges – between men's true or rational interests and their apparent, diseased, limited interests which are not to be counted as providing moral norms. Allied with this is the distinction, common in Marxist propaganda, between real 'needs' and mere irrational desires. Morality, in other words, is based on what men want, but we are to include only their rational, real (read approved?) wants. This is as true

49

for the metaphysical Marxian humanist, with his rationalist conception of what is fitting for man, and his ultimately arbitrary singling out of some potentialities in place of others, as it is for the more empirical 'materialist'. Both, in concentrating attention on the practical tasks of social transformation, have tended to deal very cavalierly indeed with the moral presuppositions on which their support for such transformations is based. Thus we find the ethic of human self-realisation, a doctrine of what is proper or fitting for man, the alleged demands of enlightened self-interest and utilitarianism all floating about in loose, unsupported formulations – as though these conceptions had no history of discussion and criticism in moral philosophy.

There is, I think, a reason for all this. The type of views examined in this chapter attempt to avoid the problems of moral philosophy by appealing to what are allegedly common human demands, rejected only by the pathological. In doing so, the writers in question reduce ethics to politics (make it a matter of 'common consent', or counting heads) and import into ethical discussion the techniques characteristic of the political agitator. The moral philosopher is concerned with distinctions and with logical difficulties – for him, one exception to an allegedly universal rule is as fatal as ten thousand exceptions. His language is designed for precision, for bringing out the exact basis of disagreement; the politician's language tends to obscure issues in order to elicit consent. Marxist moral philosophy or ethical discussion, especially in recent years, has tended to vague proclamations of welfare and satisfaction and self-realisation of the individual as goals that all rational people pursue. In doing so, it has had more in common with election speeches than with moral philosophy or scientific enquiry. Just as the post-war enthusiasm for 'welfare' tended (on the theoretical side) to obscure all real problems and conflicts, to merge all sciences into one science and to gloss over the distinctions between policies and between men, so the Marxian appeal to what men really want, to human satisfaction and self-realisation, depends on the constant use of vague and morally loaded terms in an attempt to suggest agreement where there is in fact disagreement, unanimity where there is conflict. (This, incidentally, is why the utilitarianism of Marxists is normally negative utilitarianism – it seems even to them more plausible to say that all men want to remove suffering than to say that they pursue 'happiness'.) The philosopher's concern with examining in detail such terms as 'happiness', 'satisfaction', 'suffering' and 'interest' is entirely absent from Marxist writing.

One sociological point is worth adding. The illusion of a common interest, the notion that men all basically pursue the same thing, is most plausible at times of crisis, war, revolution, etc., when large sections of society feel that they face a fundamental, wide-ranging threat or impediment which must be removed before they can engage in or further any of their varied pursuits. It loses its plausibility in times of stability, when men resume a wider range of activities. We shall see in the next chapter how the recognition of moral complexity, and of the difficulty of moral philosophy, develops among Soviet philosophers precisely as Soviet society moves from crude war-time conditions to comparative stability and complexity, to the recognition that there is more than one interest in society, that planning can never be total and that human longings and aims conflict, both internally in the one person and as between one person and another. Co-operation and division are equally parts of human and of social life.

Soviet Marxism–Leninism and its philosophy of dialectical materialism occupy a special, controversial, place in the history and theory of Marxian and Marxist thought. Officially, the Communist Party of the Soviet Union has seen itself as standing in true apostolic succession to Marx and Engels. It has devoted much effort to sponsoring and controlling (as a task of fundamental *political* importance) the propagation of a Marxist–Leninist philosophy, grounded in the classics of Marxism, allegedly representing a coherent and systematic Marxist view of the world. Soviet Marxism has become a pervasive official ideology of the Soviet State, taught in schools and universities as the only truly 'scientific' world outlook, deviation from which is at best an error and at worst a counter-revolutionary act. Sympathisers have claimed that the Soviet Union is the only country in which, for fifty years, a vast collective effort has gone into the study, systematisation and popularisation of Marxist thought; the results, therefore, should be viewed as those of a devoted and coherent school of Marxists, bringing many informed minds and a wealth of theoretical and practical experience to bear on each problem of Marxist philosophy. To most non-Communists, however, including social democratic Marxists, the realities of Soviet life and the theoretical constructions of Soviet philosophers have seemed a vicious and vulgar caricature of Marxist thought. The Russian Bolsheviks after 1917, they would say, transformed Marxism into a dogmatic theology meant to justify one-party rule and to establish ideological control over a backward peasant society. This theology was organised around 'sacred texts' (the works of Marx, Engels, Lenin and for a period Stalin) and an ecclesiastical authority that may not be challenged (the Communist Party of the Soviet Union); it recognised official teachers (the approved Party ideologists) and provoked or invented innumerable heresies sought out and persecuted as such. Not only did all this falsify the whole spirit of Marx's life and work, not only was it premised on the un-Marxian notion of a dictatorship *over* the proletariat in place of a dictatorship *of* the proletariat, but in making Marxist thought totally subservient to the day-to-day practical requirements and internecine power struggles of the Soviet régime it simply killed genuine critical Marxist thought and substituted philistine dogma and pseudo-philosophy for criticism and rationality.

Certainly, Soviet philosophy as an allegedly authoritative guide to Marxian thought has to be approached with great suspicion. The conditions of pervasive censorship, long coupled with the vicious use of political terror and political denunciation, successfully destroyed any public manifestation of independence or integrity on the part of Soviet philosophers as a body; we know that for many years they wrote and taught as they were ordered to write and teach. Even in the comparatively relaxed condition after Stalin, we still cannot be satisfied that the books published by Soviet philosophers in the Soviet Union today accurately reflect what they themselves believe. The Soviet philosopher suffers from the internal censorship set up by his own sense of prudence and the external censorship made ubiquitous by a police State, not to speak of the more general effects of the deliberate politicalisation and popularisation of philosophical thought.[24] Further, as Dr Z. A. Jordan has recently attempted to show in detail in his book *The Evolution of Dialectical Materialism* (London, 1967), the systematisation of Marxism popularised under the name of 'dialectical materialism' does not stem directly from Marx himself. It deviates from his attitudes in quite fundamental respects, it has gone through periods of evolution in which basic assumptions have been reinterpreted to produce substantial shifts in position. The creators of 'dialectical materialism' were Engels, Plekhanov, Lenin, Deborin, Stalin and the ideological commissions of the C.P.S.U., whose attitudes, concerns and ability were often very far removed from those of Marx himself, and, in various respects, from each other's.

Nevertheless, the consideration of Soviet Marxism–Leninism

and its view (or rather its successive views) on ethics has a certain point. A vulgarisation *can* help to illuminate a doctrine, both by bringing out more sharply its initial lacunae and inconsistencies, and by reminding us of the practical consequences to which it can lead. Dr Israel Getzler, in his biographical study of the Menshevik leader Martov (*Martov*, Melbourne U.P., 1967), shows us the moral disgust that Martov and other Menshevik leaders felt when faced, especially between 1903 and 1918, by Lenin's unscrupulous tactics and lack of nicety in moral matters (the scandal of the Schmidt inheritance and Lenin's connection with counterfeiting and bank robberies to augment Party funds are the best known instances). They felt, very deeply, that the Party of the Revolution must itself set a moral example – but, as Dr Getzler shows, they had the greatest difficulty in arguing this, in putting up an ethical counter-position, *from within Marxism*, while being still unwilling to go outside it. It is, indeed, the shifts in Communist attitudes to morality that we shall find especially instructive, while noting – as I shall argue below – that Communist thinkers have made no contribution to resolving the *problems* that Marxist pronouncements on ethics create.

Soviet Marxism–Leninism is an ideology. 'Generally speaking', as Professor Kichitaro Katsuda has recently put it,[25] 'a political ideology consists of three elements – first, a goal, a future image, or an ideal which it puts forth as the aim of the political movement or political power; secondly, an analysis and judgment of the given political situations on which policies and programmes of the political power or movement should be founded; and thirdly, a philosophy or myth to justify the formation of the party or political power.' Soviet Marxism–Leninism was able to draw from classical Marxism in quite a direct way two of the components needed – the utopian vision of the future Communist society which was the ultimate justification of the whole struggle and the Marxist analysis and critique of the class society showing that the 'old world' was both doomed and unworthy of preservation. On the ethical side, the utopian vision took up the ethic of the spontaneously co-operative, free and unalienated man, while the critique of bourgeois civilisation placed special emphasis on the 'materialist' critique of morality, on the 'exposure' of moral codes as serving class interests. The third element – the philosophy or myth justifying the Party's seizure of power and the Party dictatorship – was provided by the specifically Leninist component in Bolshevism, the elevation of the Communist Party and its cadre of professional revolutionaries as the mouthpiece of history and the representatives of 'consciousness'. It was this element which provided, on the ethical side, the notoriously end-directed ethic of Leninism – the good is that which promotes the power of the Party and hence the coming or consolidation of the Revolution; it is that which is 'on the side of history'. In the historical development of Bolshevism, as of political Marxism more generally, we shall find a historically conditioned tendency to emphasise, at various times, one element of this triad at the expense of others, coupled, however, with an attempt to keep all the options open and so to prevent the system from tearing apart in an obvious way. We shall first examine here the morality, or moral pronouncements, associated with each of these elements and then consider the way in which Soviet philosophers, as part of the recent revival of moral philosophy, have attempted to build them into a coherent philosophical ethic.

The utopian element in Russian Marxism reached its peak, as one might have expected, in the period just preceding and just following the Revolution itself. It drew, quite heavily, on religious messianic and nihilist traditions – the Revolution was to be a bloody act of purification, a total destruction of the Old World and the inauguration of a radically new society and a radically new set of human relationships. This is the theme of Alexander Blok's famous poem, 'The Twelve', where the true Christ is seen emerging from the destruction, rapine and profanity of Revolution. It was, it should be said, always stronger among 'free intellectuals' sympathetic to the Revolution than among Communists who had subjected themselves to the discipline of the Leninist Communist Party and were already concerned to impose a similar discipline on the whole society. Thus those whom Professor G. L. Kline has called the Nietzschean Russian Marxists[26] – Vol'ski, Lunacharsky, Bogdanov and Bazarov – writing at the beginning of the twentieth century held out the vision of the fully human, self-determined man in whom the conflict of individual and society has been completely overcome, and whose life is devoted to the creative mastery of things and the creative expression of human capacities. Lunacharsky and Vol'ski, as Professor Kline has reminded us, saw the free, creative *individual* as the basis of the new morality: the bourgeoisie had freed the individual in the hour of Revolution only to enslave him in the hour of triumph, the proletariat would command the individual in the hour of Revolution only to free him in the hour of triumph. Bogdanov and Bazarov, on the other hand, put primary emphasis on the collective, but as a spontaneous fusion of individuals, as an ecstatic religious commune in which 'our tiny being disappears, is fused with the infinite'. While there was some attempt to link this morality with the proletariat, it was with the proletariat as the most suffering and revolutionary class, as the class that would destroy the old world of property and individualism, and thereby purify man and society. To all the Nietzscheans, morality in the truly Communist society would be a spontaneous, artistic expression of human nature – external norms and obligations would disappear.

All this, however, stood on the very edge of Marxist thought in Russia and did not long survive the realities of the New Society. Bogdanov, Bazarov and Vol'ski fell into disfavour from the moment of the Revolution; Lunacharsky, who served as the first People's Commissar for Culture, followed them the moment Bolshevik orthodoxy became more rigid. Those who were genuinely concerned with ethics among Russian revolutionaries invariably went outside Marxism – the group we have mentioned to Nietzsche, another group (Berdyaev, Struve and Bulgakov during their 'Marxist' phase) to Kant. Within Marxism there was all too little to build on. The true intellectual guardians of Marxist orthodoxy in Russia – G. V. Plekhanov, L. I. Akselrod (-Ortodoks) and A. M. Deborin – characteristically took little interest in ethics and ethical theory. What little they did say on the subject was an eclectic mixture of Marx, Engels, Spinoza and Kautsky. Lenin, the ultimately successful guardian, was, as Professor Kline has put it,[27] 'a pure Machiavellian in the technical sense of the term: he systematically subordinated questions of individual and social morality to the tactical problem of the acquisition and maintenance of power. "Our morality", he declared in 1920, "is wholly subordinated to the interests of the class struggle of the proletariat." ' These words were echoed by Trotsky, Zalkind and the few other Party men who devoted any attention to ethics at that time. Nevertheless, certain aspects of the truly human ethic foreseen by Marx and in a less thoroughgoing way by Engels did become part of the utopian component even of official Marxist–Leninist ideology. The abolition of private property, exploitation and class conflict, it was argued, would produce a society in which the social and the individual interest came to coincide – the worker, by the conditions of his life in the factory and through his involvement in revolutionary struggle, was already the bearer of a new morality of co-operation, mutual help and dedication to a common cause. When all mankind became workers, when the very memory of private property and class distinctions had ceased to exist, the State, the police force, the bourgeois family, crime and self-seeking would wither away. So would external moral rules and sanctions. Disputes, as Lenin had said, would be settled on the spot, among comrades, the individual and the collective would be one. In the transitional period, however, all the emphasis was first on the Party and then on the collective. The educational theories of A. S. Makarenko, the conduct of Soviet schools and of the Communist Party cells, and Party propaganda generally all stressed the subordination of the individual to the demands of the group, his duty to submit to its criticism and to identify himself with its will. At the theoretical level, the precise nature of the group will and its relation to the wills of the individuals composing it were never examined; at the practical level, the group became the vehicle for the transmission of Party requirements and Party demands, handed down from above.

In the period between 1920 and 1936 – a period of the consolidation of Soviet power, and after 1928 of the attempt to impose a harsh labour discipline and harsh material sacrifices on a reluctant population – both the truly human ethic of freedom and the utilitarian ethic of individual satisfaction were increasingly relegated to the utopian future, while Leninist Machiavellianism and the priority of the collective formed the content of the 'socialist' morality of the present. This was the period in which Trotsky, in connection with terrorism and the civil war, denounced the 'Kantian-clerical', vegetarian-Quaker chatter about the 'sanctity of human life', in which M. I. Kalinin (then and later a sort of moral sage for the peasant and the worker) wrote: 'Our morality consists in this: all that which helps to strengthen the working class, its might in battle and the course of socialist construction, all that, without question, is obligatory for the Komsomol and the member of the Communist Party, all that he must do, all that is his moral duty.'[28] In the socialist society, Makarenko wrote:

there should be no isolated individual, either protruding in the shape of a pimple or ground into dust on the roadway, but a member of a socialist collective. . . . The individual personality assumes a new position in the educational process – it is not the object of educational influence, but its carrier. It becomes its subject, but it becomes its subject only by expressing the interests of the entire collective.[29]

The positive content of socialist morality was thus turned into a form of labour discipline – emphasis on the 'duty' to work, the 'moral' value of toil, obedience to the collective, devotion to the Soviet Union, socialism and the working class, hatred for its enemies, readiness to give up one's self for economic upbuilding or the victory of socialism. Thus the first, utopian component of Marxist ideology was gradually reinterpreted to become a theoretical base for the third, Leninist component of the ideology – it became a morality of dedicated obedience and social conformity, a vehicle for Party power and Party control.

Neither have Soviet writers made any significant theoretical contribution to the materialist critique of moralities, initially linked with the second, critical element in Marxist–Leninist ideology. Soviet criticism and analysis of bourgeois society has been notable mainly for its crudity, vulgarity and frequent intellectual dishonesty: fifty years of Soviet philosophy have produced nothing that can be regarded as an interesting economic or social interpretation of a philosophical thinker or of a philosophical school of thought worthy to rank beside Francis Cornford's *From Religion to Philosophy* or E. B. Pashukanis's attempt to link civil law with the assumptions requisite for the operation of a market. The relationship between moral philosophy and the class structure of a society, though constantly proclaimed by Soviet philosophers, has not been brought out in any interesting or illuminating way. On the whole, Soviet philosophers have gone little further than linking discrete moral attitudes with class prejudices: Aristotle's contempt for slaves and women, Locke's concern with property and – at a somewhat more general level – the concern with hierarchy in 'feudal' philosophy and the growth of individualism and the assertion of individual rights as the bourgeois market begins to take over. The latter, of course, are sound points, but the Soviet periodisation of philosophy into slave-owning, feudal and bourgeois eras has tended to simplify and vulgarise their application. At the same time, the concern with periodisation and linking everything to a specific class-outlook has tended to obscure the genuine logical concerns of moral philosophers; it has led to the conflation of questions of form and content, of moral philosophy with moral attitudes. The very strong insistence on organising the whole history of philosophy around the allegedly fundamental dispute between materialism and idealism (between those who treat matter as primary and those who treat consciousness as primary) has proved particularly unilluminating in the history of ethics, where disputes and difficulties have cut right across this issue – if it was, indeed, ever an important issue in any branch of philosophy. The dispute on the relationship of 'ought' and 'is', for instance, which Soviet philosophers handle particularly badly, and the whole problem of establishing moral *obligation* are not connected with the question at issue between 'materialism' (realism, or naturalism?) and idealism. Soviet philosophers have thus far not got to grips with the real problems in the history of moral philosophy and have not contributed significantly to the understanding of this history. On the internal side, in relation to Soviet morality, the materialist critique of ethics was for a period used primarily to make moral and ethical questions subsidiary to the fulfilment of the Five-Year Plans and the tasks of socialist construction. It thus became a further prop for the end-directed ethic of the Leninist Party. It was through economic achievements and economic sacrifice that the truly human morality would ultimately be achieved, the argument ran; therefore, in the meantime, moral judgments have no independent force or significance.

In 1936, with the proclamation of the Stalin Constitution and the announcement that Soviet society had entered upon socialism, the doctrine of the primacy of the economic gave way to a new emphasis on stability and the moral and legal foundations of a socialist society. Normative law and normative morality were no longer seen as hang-overs from a capitalist past or as transitional measures in a period of struggle and construction – they were given a creative role in building the society of the future. (Dialectical materialism was reinterpreted accordingly.) Steps were taken to strengthen the family and respect for law as lasting social phenomena; increasing emphasis was put on the relatively independent force and role of morality as a set of norms for socialist living in a socialist society. The terrible purges and the Second World War limited the impact of this development for a period, but did not halt it. From 1946 onward, an increasing emphasis on Marxist ethics and Communist morality came to be felt; in 1951, a conference of Soviet and Czech philosophers agreed that the teaching of Marxist ethics was inadequate and confused and that specialist courses should be created. From that time onward, there has been a steady growth of both low-level moral exhortation and somewhat higher-level philosophical discussion in ethics. The number of articles and books, at both levels, has grown enormously. Quantitatively, at least, there is no longer an ethical lacuna in Soviet Marxism; if anything there is an unusually high degree of moralism for a modern society. (Soviet child-bearing manuals *advocate* the temporary, ostentatious withdrawal of love, refusal to 'play speaks', putting on of a sullen expression, etc., to show the offending child that it has wounded its parents in being 'selfish' – i.e. disobedient.)

The main theme that has come out of all this moral and

moralising activity, then, is the taking up of a frankly normative stand. In the last fifteen years – especially since the Twenty-Second Congress of the Communist Party of the Soviet Union in 1961 adopted 'the moral code of the builder of Communism' – the Marxist exposure of all normative morality as mere ideology or class interest disappeared from Soviet writing. A great deal of emphasis is now placed on such familiar normative ethical concepts of 'bourgeois' morality as conscience, duty, etc. The normative bindingness of Socialist morality as the truly human morality is constantly proclaimed. Its content, as listed in the new programme of the Communist Party, is devotion to the Communist cause, love of the socialist motherland and the other socialist countries, conscientious labour for the good of society, concern for the preservation and growth of public wealth (i.e. state property), a high sense of public duty and intolerance of actions harmful to the public interest, collectivism and comradely mutual assistance, humane relations between and mutual respect for individuals, honesty and truthfulness, moral purity, modesty and unpretentiousness in social and private life, mutual respect in the family and an uncompromising attitude to injustice, parasitism, dishonesty, careerism and money-grubbing, etc., etc.

'In the years of the cult of personality', the new Soviet *History of Philosophy* now says,[30] 'the inhuman, amoral character of a series of actions by Stalin and those closely associated with him – the infringement of legality, the repressive measures directed against honest people and even whole nationalities, the separation from the needs of the toilers – inflicted serious harm on the Communist education of the toilers. All this retarded the scientific working out of ethical problems.' Certainly, in reaction against the harsh inhumanity of the Stalin régime, there is now a strong tendency to emphasise certain moral values as having intrinsic worth – such values as honesty, sincerity, family love, truthfulness, etc. This has resulted in a growing interest, on the part of less servile Soviet philosophers, in the philosophy of values, in a desire to see ethics, like aesthetics, grounded on a set of categories and distinctions comparatively independent of politics. The result is that the present official systematisation of Marxist ethics, in trying to reflect various trends in the Soviet Union, is beginning to vacillate between a makeshift and eclectic view and a reactionary attempt (expressed by such 'philosophers' as Mitin, Fedoseyev and Shishkin) to maintain the older dogmatism in slightly less offensive form.

The formal position, as set out in the growing number of textbooks on Marxist–Leninist ethics designed for university use, runs something like this: Morality is the totality of norms governing the attitudes of men to one another and to society. These norms arise in consequence of social needs, and vary with fundamental changes in social relationships. In societies divided into classes, the social interest confronts the individual as an external, hostile force, in conflict with his individual interest. Further, the alleged representatives of the social interest – the ruling classes – put forward as the social interest what are in fact sectional interests, class interests, which call forth competing assertions of *their* class interests from the exploited. We thus have, in class societies, competing moralities. The moralities of the exploited classes, however, as the moralities of the overwhelming majority of mankind, contain some elements of a general, social interest which has been common to all periods. There is also moral value in the morality of classes that are or were 'progressive' in their time. In Communist-led societies, where private ownership and the class structure dependent on it have been abolished, the social interest, however, has become the conscious interest of the whole people. The individual and the social interest therefore here coalesce and true (unideological) morality becomes possible. Conscience and duty are the individual's subjective internalisation of the social interest, his recognition of his interdependence with his fellow-men. Under socialism, they provide man with moral norms that society sets before him, distinguished from legal norms only by the absence of physical sanctions.

These norms have so far not been discussed in Soviet philosophy at any level approaching logical, philosophical respectability. The precise nature and foundation of the social interest have not been examined and its relation to individual interests is consistently obscured. (The fact that the social interest both does

62

and does not coincide with the individual interest is treated as an example of 'dialectical unity', which is to restate and not to solve the problem.) The social interest and the demand of the collective are not reduced to a summation of individual interests – yet the well-being of man is constantly presented as the fundamental norm of Communist morality. Here a passage from the Soviet philosopher S. Utkin may be cited as representative of the level of analysis:

> It is part of every man's character to have an internal striving to be better, morally purer, spiritually richer. And this is the command of his conscience, which represents the dictates, first of all, of his closest social surroundings, of the feeling of responsibility before the collective in which he lives and works, before those nearest and dearest to him whose authority and opinion are the highest unwritten law for him.[31]

This running together, without serious examination and without any real supporting argument, of a particular individual's aspirations, of the 'needs' of society and the dictates of the social environment, and of the demands of other individuals, is completely characteristic of the Soviet discussion of morality in the socialist society.

At the same time, mainly as a result of certain political pronouncements by N. S. Khrushchev and the Twenty-First Congress of the C.P.S.U., there is now some emphasis on the universally human moral values of earlier ages, the so-called 'simple norms' of morality and justice, which were distorted in the society of exploitation, or not genuinely applied, but nevertheless even there recognised as having moral value. On the basis of these norms, Soviet philosophers are attempting to build up a system of *categories* of morality – such as justice, good, honour, conscience, duty and happiness, to take the categories nominated by L. A. Arkhangel'ski in his book *The Categories of Marxist Ethics* (Moscow, 1963). These they see as independent in form, if not in content, of the specific economic base of a given society. This, of course, comes extremely close to an axiology and there is, understandably enough, a revival of interest in the Soviet Union in the work of Nikolai Hartmann. The striking thing in all this is the disintegration of any coherent or distinctive Marxian view in ethics and the attempt to come back into some sort of main stream of normative ethical thought. Thus the Leningrad philosopher, V. P. Tugarinov, in his book *On the Values of Life and Culture* (Leningrad, 1960) turns his attention to such traditional values as truth, good and beauty and tries to go beyond the conception of duty (too strongly emphasised in Soviet ethics, he complains) to a conception of objective values, grounded in human nature itself (see especially p. 125). 'Good', he writes in terms all too reminiscent of 'bourgeois' philosophy, 'is benefit for people, for society, brought about *consciously*, with the aim of bringing about benefit' (Tugarinov's italics, p. 124). Truth, beauty and education are good because people are so constituted as to pursue them and to derive pleasure from them.

In a very recent article, the now somewhat discredited doyen of Soviet Party philosophers, Academician M. V. Mitin, writes:[32]

> Either Marxism as a whole and Marxist philosophy in particular will retain all of their critical revolutionary substance, their inner ideological purity and *wholeness*, and will develop according to the teaching of Marx, Engels and Lenin, or they will take the path of eclecticism and dissolve in a profusion of bourgeois and petty-bourgeois doctrines, superficially taking something from scientific communism but being in principle deeply hostile to it.

In forty years of philosophical activity, Mitin and his colleagues failed completely to work out a respectable coherent Marxist position in ethics, or even to address themselves to the real problems of the subject. In so far as Soviet philosophers are beginning to do genuine moral philosophy today (and they have yet to make any real or independent contribution to it), they are taking 'the path of eclecticism'.

VII. CONCLUSION

The difficulty that men – and moral philosophers – have encountered in trying 'to give ethics a foundation' stems primarily from the mixture of description and advocacy characteristic of moral claims. Emphasis on the prescriptive or advocative functions of moral statements constantly threatens to turn them into arbitrary commands; emphasis on their descriptive content invites disagreement and robs them of their normative force. Moral philosophers, despite Hume, have thus been tempted, consciously or unconsciously, to conflate the descriptive and prescriptive by using such key but unexamined moral concepts as 'value', 'pleasure', 'human nature', etc. The great progress made in moral philosophy in the last fifty years has not led to any convincing solution of its basic problems, but it has enabled us to see much more clearly how these problems arise. Moral philosophy, in this century, has passed through a vital stage of the clarification of issues, of the careful examination of the structure of moral language and the function of moral terms. Karl Marx lived and wrote before this important development took place; virtually all of his disciples have been unable to profit by it. At a time when competent philosophers have come carefully to distinguish the advocative or normative element in moral claims and disputes from the empirical, descriptive element, Marxists still insist on treating morality or moralities as undifferentiated wholes, running together their content, function and origin, devoting no attention to the character of moral arguments or moral justification, refusing to study the logic of moral disputes.

The failure to pay serious attention to questions of logic and to linguistic precision is the main reason why it is impossible to speak of a serious Marxist contribution to ethical philosophy. Soviet philosophers, for instance, attack sharply what they call the 'positivist' erection of a dichotomy between 'ought' and 'is'. But their argument against separating the prescriptive and the descriptive invariably misses the point. It is perfectly true that demands are themselves facts, historical empirical occurrences, and that any 'ought-claim' will be grounded in such an empirical demand or principle. But the point is what function such demands or commands or principles perform in argument, whether they can be deduced from 'neutral' descriptions containing no demands or requirements, whether they can be 'refuted' or only opposed, disobeyed or ignored. In their attempt to ground morality in demands or requirements that everyone accepts (a very traditional move), Marxists, if anything, exceed the imprecision of traditional philosophers – the requirements of 'human nature' (sometimes real, sometimes ideal), social requirements, the requirements of art and culture as productive activities and the requirement of history are all run together without serious examination. This imprecision, I would argue, is necessary for anyone seeking to establish norms as though they were prescribed by the nature of society, or man, or human life. But the same imprecision arises on the critical side, in the materialist exposure of moralities. Even when Marxists treat moralities as not binding, as sets of sectional demands, they are unclear – to others and to themselves – precisely what sort of demands are in question, where they originate and what they seek.

In the field of ethics, then, Marx himself may be regarded as a social critic rather than as a moral philosopher. His argument, it is true, was directed primarily against authoritarian moralities seeking to blind man in the name of alleged moral 'laws' and his attention was devoted primarily to the lack of correspondence between social reality and alleged moral ideals. His own moral ideal – free, conscious and spontaneous co-operation between individuals – he took for granted; his concern was with removing those social conditions which, he believed, stood in the way of its realisation. His followers have on the whole maintained the habit of confusing problems of moral philosophy with problems of social reform. They claim as a virtue, instead of recognising as a theoretical defect, that they devote their attention to conditions that stand in the way of human happiness instead of asking precisely what 'happiness' means.

All this is not to say that Marx has made no contribution whatever to the discussion of ethics in modern philosophy. It was he who pointed the way to a sociology of morals, to the recognition of moral codes and moral principles as social products, formed in specific social contexts, derived from human activities and human and social demands. He has thus greatly increased our sophistication in talking about morals and he has enabled others – sociologists, anthropologists and psychologists – to increase it still further. But the problem in ethics has been the relevance of empirical information to ethical systems and moral claims, to the problems of moral philosophy. Until the logical analysis we have seen in the past fifty years was accomplished, this question could not be seriously considered. There is still sufficient disagreement among moral philosophers to make the very subject-matter of ethics a matter of dispute. But in so far as the points at issue are being narrowed down, and grasped more clearly, the philosophy of morals can once more be brought into conjunction with the sociology and psychology of morals. Moral philosophers might now recognise that there are empirical problems still outstanding, the relevance of which can now be discussed more fruitfully. The logic of moral discourse has had adequate examination, for the time being at least. Perhaps we should turn to some of the problems Marx left unsolved and that his followers have not tried to consider – what is the precise social or human empirical content of various moralities; if moralists have not been making mere empty noises, or random demands, what *have* they been talking about, what *sort* of demands do they make, *what* have they considered morally relevant and *why*? If ethics is concerned with the conditions of co-operation, what *are* the possible types of co-operation, how do their conditions vary? Are 'rules' connected with people, or with activities – is ethics concerned with individuals or ways of life? It is in these areas that a sensitivity to history and to social questions, such as Marx had, is invaluable to the moral philosopher.

NOTES

1. D. Riazanov *et al.* (eds.), *Marx–Engels Gesamtausgabe* (Berlin–Moscow, 1927 f.) section 1, vol. 5, p. 227.

2. The sharp division between Marx and Engels which needs to be made when dealing with their theoretical work is now increasingly accepted in serious scholarly work, but still seems to occasion surprise and resentment in some circles. Suffice it here to recall the words written by Joseph Schumpeter when he found himself making the same division: 'I observe that the few comments on Engels that are contained in this sketch ["Marx as an Economist"] are of a derogatory nature. This is unfortunate and not due to any intention to belittle the merits of that eminent man. I do think, however, that it should be frankly admitted that intellectually and especially as a theorist he stood far below Marx. We cannot even be sure that he always got the latter's meaning. His interpretations must therefore be used with care.' – Joseph A. Schumpeter, *Capitalism, Socialism and Democracy* (4th edn, London, 1959) p. 39.

3. See, for instance, the famous passage in Marx's Preface to the first edition of *Capital*, vol. 1, where Marx insists that the capitalist and the landowner, though portrayed in a far from rosy light in his work, are considered only as personifications of economic categories, as carriers of class relationships and class interests. The individual, Marx adds, cannot be made responsible for conditions of which he is the creature. In general terms, Marx's view here and elsewhere implies that systems, not people, are the objects of moral judgment.

4. Eugene Kamenka, *The Ethical Foundations of Marxism* (London, New York, 1962) p. vii.

5. Karl Popper, *The Open Society and Its Enemies* (London, 1957) vol. II, p. 199.

6. Herbert Marcuse, *Eros and Civilization* (London, 1956) pp. 109–10.

7. The revolutionary implications of the Kantian philosophy have been least appreciated in England, where interest in Kant has centred on the logical and epistemological concerns of the *Critique of Pure Reason* as attempts to overcome the discrete atomism of Humean empiricism and where the discussion of Kant's moral philosophy has concentrated on the concepts of duty and inclination. At the personal level, Englishmen have seen Kant as a model of Protestant decorum.

Only recently, through the work of such Continentally trained historians of philosophy as Ernst Cassirer, has the radical impact of Kant's thought been appreciated.

8. For an attempt to document this development, see Eugene Kamenka, *The Ethical Foundations of Marxism*, esp. pp. 17–86.

9. Ludwig Feuerbach, *The Essence of Christianity*, trans. by Marian Evans (New York, 1957) p. 270.

10. A. M. Deborin, *Ludwig Feuerbach* (Moscow, 1923) p. 207. This, the final sentence of the book, was dropped from the 1929 reprint; less than two years later, Deborin was condemned, in part, for failing to emphasise sufficiently the creative leap between Marx and Feuerbach.

11. Robert C. Tucker, *Philosophy and Myth in Karl Marx* (Cambridge U.P., 1961).

12. Maximilien Rubel, 'Le concept de démocratie chez Marx', in *Contrat Social*, vol. VI, No. 4.

13. Karl Marx, 'On the Jewish Question', in *Marx–Engels Gesamtausgabe*, sec. I, vol. I, sub-vol. i, p. 603, or in Karl Marx, *Early Writings*, trans. and ed. by T. B. Bottomore (London, 1963) p. 37.

14. Karl Marx, *Economico-Philosophical Manuscripts* in *Marx–Engels Gesamtausgabe*, sec. I, vol. 3, pp. 111–12, in *Early Writings*, p. 153; Karl Marx, *Grundrisse der Kritik der politischen Ökonomie* (Berlin, 1953) p. 505.

15. Adam Schaff, *A Philosophy of Man* (New York, 1963) p. 84.

16. For a detailed discussion of Engels's account of truth, see John Anderson, 'Marxist Philosophy', in *Australasian Journal of Psychology and Philosophy* (1935), pp. 24 ff., esp. pp. 26–32.

17. Eugene Kamenka, 'Marxism and the History of Philosophy', in John Passmore (ed.) *The Historiography of the History of Philosophy* (Supplement 5 to *History and Theory*, The Hague, 1965) pp. 83–104, esp. pp. 87–8; and Eugene Kamenka, *The Ethical Foundations of Marxism*, pp. 134–42.

18. I. N. Lushchitski *et al.* (eds.) *Osnovy marksistsko–leninskoi etiki* (*Foundations of Marxist–Leninist Ethics*) (Minsk, 1965) p. 17.

19. Adam Schaff, *A Philosophy of Man*, pp. 132–3.

20. Howard Selsam, *Ethics and Progress* (New York, 1965) p. 13.

21. Op. cit. p. 10.

22. Donald Clark Hodges, 'Marx's Ethics and Ethical Theory', in Ralph Miliband and John Saville (eds.) *The Socialist Register 1964* (London, 1964) pp. 227–41.

23. Op. cit. p. 238.

24. For a description of the conditions under which Soviet philosophers have worked, and of the resultant cynicism and dishonesty, see Eugene Kamenka, 'Soviet Philosophy – 1917–1967' in A. Simirenko (ed.) *Contemporary Soviet Social Thought* (Chicago, 1968), and Eugene

Kamenka, 'Philosophers in Moscow' in *Survey – Journal of Soviet and East European Studies* (1967), no. 62, pp. 15–24.

25. Kichitaro Katsuda, 'Dilemmas of the Soviet Totalitarian System', in *Review – A Journal for the Study of Communism and Communist Countries* (Tokyo, 1965) no. 6, pp. 1–2.

26. See G. L. Kline, 'Changing Attitudes Toward the Individual', in C. E. Black (ed.) *The Transformation of Russian Society* (Cambridge, Mass. 1960) pp. 606–25, and G. L. Kline, 'Theoretische Ethik im russischen Frühmarxismus', in *Forschungen zur osteuropäischen Geschichte* (1963) vol. 9, pp. 269–79.

27. G. L. Kline, 'Soviet Morality, Current' in V. Ferm (ed.) *The Encyclopedia of Morals* (New York, 1956) at p. 570. The point that the ethic of Plekhanov and his disciples is an eclectic mixture of Marx, Engels, Spinoza and Kautsky has also been emphasised by Kline.

28. Cited from M. I. Kalinin, *O kommunisticheskom vospitanii* (*On Communist Education*) (Moscow, 1958) p. 93. The frequency with which Kalinin is cited in Soviet writing on the 1920s today does not reflect his importance at the time, but only the fact that he is one of the few Old Bolsheviks who have not become un-persons through association with the disgraced, i.e. Trotsky, Bukharin and, finally, Stalin.

29. Cited from A. S. Makarenko, *Sochineniya* (*Works*) 7 vols. (Moscow, 1950–2) vol. 5, p. 333; vol. 2, p. 403.

30. M. A. Dynnik *et al.* (eds.) *Istoriya filosofii* (*History of Philosophy*), 6 vols. (Moscow, 1957–65) vol. VI, book 1, p. 478.

31. S. Utkin, *Ocherki po marksistsko–leninskoi etike* (*Notes on Marxist–Leninist Ethics*) (Moscow, 1962) p. 300.

32. M. V. Mitin, 'Razvitie dialekticheskogo materializma v posleoktyabrskuyu epokhu' ('The Development of Dialectical Materialism in the Post-October Epoch') in *Voprosy filosofii* (1968), No. 1, p. 23.

BIBLIOGRAPHY

(Books are listed only once, under the heading to which they are primarily relevant, but often contain material bearing on other sections. Foreign language works, with the exception of Dr Rubel's invaluable anthology, have been excluded.)

GENERAL BACKGROUND

Berlin, I., *Karl Marx – His Life and Environment* (3rd edn, New York, 1963).

Burns, E. (ed.) *A Handbook of Marxism* (New York, 1935).

Kamenka, E., *Karl Marx* (London, 1969 – forthcoming).

Lichtheim, G., *Marxism: An Historical and Critical Study* (London, New York, 1961).

Marx, K., *Pages choisies pour une éthique socialiste*, ed. M. Rubel (Paris, 1948).

Meyer, A. G., *Marxism: The Unity of Theory and Practice* (Ann Arbor, 1963).

Nicolaievsky, B., and Maenchen-Helfen, O., *Karl Marx: Man and Fighter* (London, n.d.).

Ulam, A. B., *The Unfinished Revolution* (New York, 1960).

CHAPTERS II AND III

Bell, D., *The End of Ideology*, esp. ch. 15 (rev. edn, London, New York, 1962).

Dupré, L., *The Philosophical Foundations of Marxism* (New York, 1966).

Fromm, E. (ed.) *Socialist Humanism* (New York, 1965, 1966; London, 1967).

Kamenka, E., *The Ethical Foundations of Marxism* (London, New York, 1962).

Marx, K., *Early Writings*, ed. T. B. Bottomore (London, 1963).

Tucker, R., *Philosophy and Myth in Karl Marx* (Cambridge, 1961).

CHAPTERS IV AND V

Acton, H. B., *The Illusion of the Epoch*, Part II (London, 1955; Boston, 1957).

Engels, F., *Herr Eugen Dühring's Revolution in Science (Anti-Dühring)* (New York, 1939).

—— *Ludwig Feuerbach and the Outcome of Classical German Philosophy* (numerous edns).

Kautsky, K., *Ethics and the Materialist Conception of History* (Chicago, 1918).

Marx, K., and Engels, F., *The German Ideology*, Parts I and III, ed. R. Pascal (London, 1939).

—— —— *The Communist Manifesto* (numerous edns).

Selsam, H., *Socialism and Ethics* (New York, 1949).

—— and Martel, H., *Reader in Marxist Philosophy*, Parts V and VII (New York, 1963).

—— *Ethics and Progress* (New York, 1965).

Venable, V., *Human Nature: The Marxian View* (London, 1946).

CHAPTER VI

Contributions in the journal *Studies in Soviet Thought* (Fribourg 1961–) esp. by Richard T. De George.

Marcuse, H., *Soviet Marxism – A Critical Analysis* (London, 1958; with new preface, New York, 1961).

Programme of the Communist Party of the Soviet Union (New York, 1961).

Translations of Soviet philosophical articles in the journal *Soviet Studies in Philosophy* (New York, 1962–).

Wetter, G. A., *Dialectical Materialism: A Historical and Systematic Survey of Philosophy in the Soviet Union* (London, 1958).

—— *Soviet Ideology Today* (New York, 1966).